LOU

TENACITY
for LIFE™

LESSONS IN LIFE, BUSINESS AND THE WORLD AROUND US

TENACITY FOR LIFE

For more information, contact:

Tenacity For Life | www.tenacityforlife.com
Fig Factor Media, LLC | www.figfactormedia.com

Cover Design by DG Marco Álvarez
Layout by LDG Juan Manuel Serna Rosales

Printed in the United States of America

ISBN: 978-1-957058-26-9
Library of Congress Control Number: 2022905133

FIG
FACTOR
MEDIA

DEDICATIONS

I dedicate this book to my parents, Trinidad L. Sandoval and Berth Sandoval. Without your sacrifices I would not be here. I am forever grateful for your grace, persistence, and love. To my grandparents on both sides of the family– Gracias!

To my wife Sonia, and my daughters Sofia and Sarah– you are my everything, my inspiration. I love you so dearly. Never forget those who came before you, and remember the Tenacity within! #TeamSandoval

To my brother, sisters, and all my nieces and nephews– Never give up, the world is within your reach!

TABLE OF CONTENTS

ACKNOWLEDGMENTS

It is with Full Gratitude, and being very present to how very blessed I am, that I write this book. I stand on the shoulders of my migrant worker grandparents, the proud farmers, Virginia Godinez and Trinidad Sandoval, who came to the United States in search of a better economic situation. To my maternal grandparents, Antonio and Isabel Diaz, who left family and friends behind to find a better life. Little did they know that their grandson would one day write a book about their story and the story of their children. Little did they know the impact that that one decision–the tenacious pursuit of a better life–would have on generations to come. I am grateful for your tenacity.

To my parents, Trinidad Louis Sandoval, my man of steel who passed in 2015, and my mother, Bertha Sandoval, who due to dad's tenacity met and raised a family with many sacrifices. Mom, for all the years that you had to be the backbone of the family, raising the bunch of rambunctious kids, and the nights doing math at the kitchen table with your slow-to-catch-on son. Doing the best that they could to raise us right, educate us, and keep us on the straight and narrow. I am so glad that you, Mom, will be able to read this. Dad, I know you are smiling. Thank you so very much for your sacrifices. You were right, it was going to be ok. It always is!

I stand on the shoulders of my ancestors–this is your son, your grandson. I hope I made you proud.

I would like to thank my wife, Sonia Marie Sandoval. We

knew since the priest gave his sermon at our wedding that life would be full of many ups and downs (almost his exact words), and I'm sure at times you have wondered...but you have hung in there for eighteen years, and I know I would not change a single second of it. Not one. It is because of your love, support, and admiration that I am able to achieve and provide for our family.

To my intelligent, powerful, and beautiful daughters, Sofia Isabel and Sarah Louise, you are the light of my world. The best part of my day is when I see your faces, hear about how it went for you, and learn about your dreams. Never stop believing in yourself. Through good times and bad times (there will be some), always remember that the power to impact change is in each of you. I so look forward to seeing you continue to grow into the powerful women that I know you will be.

To my ride or die brother, Martin. We have covered so many miles on the water, and have so many to cover yet. We've come a long way since that small bedroom with bunk beds. I always appreciate you being a phone call away.

To my sister, Susana, probably the closest in level of tenacity to me, may you find your purpose, embrace it, and never let it go.

To my sister, Anabel, you've raised the first wave of college graduates in our family. Thank you for valuing education for them. So, what's next?

To my mother-in-law, Ortencia Martinez and Arturo Aguirre, you have taught me to care by your selfless support of our family through thick and thin.

To my brothers-in-law, Sergio Villagomez and Sergio Martinez, and sisters-in-law Diana and Alicia, our unsung heroes without whom all wonderful things would not be possible.

To my nieces and nephews, Xavier, Anissa, Kassan, Karizma, Caroline, Daniel, Junior, and Jacob, remember that the world is yours for the taking. Don't ever let anyone tell you otherwise, and most of all, don't settle.

To my aunts and uncles on the Sandoval side (so many) and on the Diaz side, you have all touched my lives through your actions, your patience, and your memories.

To my neighbors from the old neighborhood, the Arias family, The De La Rosa's, the Morales family, The Flores Family–I could go on... It truly did take a village!

To my Scoutmasters Mr. C, EJ, and Wally, I know I was a pain as a kid, but thank you for believing in me!

To all the mentors in my educational and professional life, many of whom I've named or anonymized in this book- Mr. Hawkins, Mr. Foster, Mr. Cappello, Mr. Derman, Dr. Breitbeil, Dr. Brauer, Dr. Libertin, Dr. Woloshek, Keith, Miles, Kim, Cynthia, Art, Felix, Jeannie, Tim, Bob, Karen, Mike L., Joe and Elaine, Jack, Thom, Mark, David, Joseph, Adam, Mark, and Ed. (I'm sure I forgot a few). Thank you!! Through your grace, patience, direction, and listening, you have made a profound difference in my professional development.

To my lifelong friends, Maurice, Alex, Brian, Rob, Lance, Mark, Jim, Art, Flex, and Pete, you have seen some highs and some lows, but you've stuck it out for the long haul, and I'm still standing.

To all my friends and colleagues at the Big Brothers Big Sisters, Boy Scouts of America, Pathways to Adventure Council, Chicago Yacht Club, RBLC, RBFF, Sail America, and YBAA, through your camaraderie I have supplemented my professional development.

To my friend Elba Aranda Suh, your support has always been a light of hope. It is through your connection that I met James Floyd and that has been a spark! Oh, and James, love you brother!

To the team at Fig Factor Media and JJR Marketing, Gaby, Marie, Lisa, Anna Marie, and the magnificent, Jackie Camacho Ruiz, TFL would not have been possible without your amazing professionalism, your patience, and grace. Bravo!!

With great gratitude, many thanks to the Board of Directors and leadership teams at Wintrust Bank, N.A, K4 Mobility, and BoatTrax, I am honored to work with you and serve alongside you!

Finally, To God, because you've always been there with me, you've never left my side and because of your grace and love—I am forever your grateful child.

Lou Sandoval

FOREWORD

Tenacity for Life, Business, and the World Around Us

"Each of us must persevere to reach our personal goal. We must learn to be tenacious, for doing so will build our character and keeps us humble." ~ **Frank Carbajal**

Approach your goals balancing tenacity with humility. When you do so, you will be better equipped to face challenges, and you will learn to be patient and when to be assertive, as you will read in Lou Sandoval's book, *Tenacity for Life.*

Lou's book delivers a powerful and inspiring message of perseverance and leadership. Naming it *Tenacity for Life* was an inspired choice as tenacity is an ingredient within our human DNA. It is also a trait that we have possessed since childhood and learn to use throughout our lives.

As you will read in Lou's journey, some of his most important leadership traits were developed during his educational upbringing and his involvement in Boy Scouts. This had a strong influence on him and encouraged his desire to pursue a STEM education and become a doctor. As he pursued the rank of Eagle Scout, Lou engaged in every science-based merit badge possible, which furthered his love for science and technology.

Lou was top of his class from grade school through high school and at DePaul University, where he majored in pre-med biochemistry. Upon graduation, as he has done throughout his life, Lou listened to his heart, talked to those he trusted, and made what might seem to be an impossible decision that would change the course of his life.

Although he was accepted at Loyola University Medical Center for medical school, he decided not to be a doctor, and instead chose pharmaceutical sales as his heart moved him to the business side of healthcare. It was tenacity that gave him this freedom to be flexible and humility that he showed when talking with the Loyola staff to explain his decision.

In *Tenacity for Life*, we can see that the spirit of embracing challenges, overcoming obstacles, and the experience of ups and downs are all meant to happen to us. Otherwise, we would not have a journey that encourages us to reach for tenacity.

In this book you will learn that within each of us are many hidden and uplifting traits. This is what will lead you to success, just as it led Lou down that path least traveled, the one that was meant just for him.

Lou Sandoval, with all his success, opens up and shares the challenges he faced and how he overcame them. He shares the secrets of his success and the tactics he used with the hope that he could help others navigate life's rough waters, all while sharing the details with honesty and humor.

Lou Sandoval is the ultimate leader and role model. He has been a mentor to many and it is this that ultimately led him to write *Tenacity for Life*. In reading this, you're letting Lou mentor you, too. Join him as he talks about relationships, business, entrepreneurship, volunteering, humanity, and what he is most proud of, starting with his children.

FRANK CARBAJAL

Founder of Silicon Valley Latino Leadership Summit

PREFACE

The genesis for *Tenacity for Life* began midway during my high school years. While some people apply yoga as a form of meditation to better focus on their life, obtain mental clarity, and visualize the harmony they seek to bring to themselves, journaling became that tool for me.

It started on spiral bound notebooks and evolved to more elaborate dime store journals that I've kept with me for many years. In these literary musings I've captured the thoughts of my adolescence, my college years and professional endeavors. It never started with the intention of creating a manuscript, although I did have the creation of a book on my bucket list.

About 10 years ago, I would select *Tenacity for Life* as the title of a blog that I created with the same intention of cataloging my various essays on experiences and thoughts.

It wasn't until the great pandemic that I sought to organize my thoughts formally into outlines which shaped the vision for the chapters that would become *Tenacity for Life*. This came out of various conversations with professionals in corporate America who felt lonely, isolated, lacking direction, and marginalized. Truth be told, a large segment was Latino. Some of these individuals felt that they did not have a voice. The tide in their work life had shifted and they felt trapped. Their question to me was always, you have been successful, have you not seen these types of problems? Success seems to come easy to you, don't you feel the struggle? You make it seem so easy.

A combination of this feedback and the great resignation, which echoed similar sentiments, led me to think that it was time to tell my story. Perhaps accumulating so many firsts in my life made it seem like I was impervious to failure, when it was quite the contrary–I channeled my failures to lift me up. It was the tenacity that fueled me. So, I began to formalize *Tenacity for Life* as a way to inspire, coach, and uplift individuals. Life can be tough; it can be unfair. YOU have the power to persevere and rise to new heights.

I have been profoundly blessed with many guiding lights throughout my life. Individuals who directly or indirectly influenced my trajectory. As a person who embraces a growth mindset, I have sought to reflect on individual experiences to find the meaning of their insertion into my life's trajectory. What were they meant to teach me? Why should I be listening?

I understand that for some who read this, you may think, wait this guy has a completely different set of problems, of the first world kind in fact. If you seek to go deeper you will see that the core of some of the challenges that I've faced stem from human interaction, the frailty of the human ego, and unmet expectations to name a few. It is in seeking beyond this superficial experience that you will find that the essence of anyone's existence is being heard, achieving reaffirmation, and feeling like they have made an impact. As human beings it is quite simple–we are a collection of experiences, our interpretation of those experiences, and how those interpretations impact our response. Our ultimate goal is choosing the appropriate response that will create the best outcome. That simple choice is fully within our control.

At the time we are living our lives, we are stuck in the muddiness of the day to day. Our experiences cloud our response at times. That is completely ok. What is incumbent upon us is to do the very best we can to positively impact those who are most important in our lives, usually our family.

In *Tenacity for Life*, I will take you on an atypical journey for a young boy with all the hopes, dreams, and aspirations of many young boys. The experiences he had, his feelings, and how they impacted the trajectory of his life. There is adversity, losses, disappointments, sickness, and loss of loved ones that fundamentally impacted his outlook on life. The values he learned from his grandparents and parents also shaped the tenacious outlook on his passions that have gotten him to many highpoints, but through many low points as well.

In reading these passages you will see that you too can overcome whichever obstacles you encounter. It is completely within the realm of possibility.

Thank you for joining me on this journey!

LOU SANDOVAL

Chicago, IL

March 2022

INTRODUCTION

"Life can only be understood backwards; but it must be lived forwards." ~ **Søren Kierkegaard**

While business had always intrigued me, my heartfelt passion was sailing. This passion made owning a boat dealership seem like the perfect opportunity to combine my two passions and the desire for entrepreneurialism and until, suddenly, one day, it was not. In fact, the business that we had worked so hard on for so many years seemed to crumble before my very eyes.

It was January of 2016 when things seemed to reach a point of no return. My dad had passed away just three days before Christmas, and I was still dealing with the toll it had taken on me. At this same time, I was managing the boat dealership that I co-owned with my business partner and best friend. We had just brought our boat dealership, Karma Yacht Sales, through the Great Recession, and we were starting to have some real challenges with our manufacturer.

Every year we participated in an annual Chicago boat show, but this year was different. Our manufacturer was pushing back, trying to put criteria around our participation that was clearly not favorable to us. Due to the recession, we were rebuilding, sales were slow in the Midwest, and we had just dealt with a similar issue in 2015. We were wary of being burned again.

We were looking for clarity on the show's financial responsibilities, but our manufacturer started pushing us. They wanted to know if we were ready to go for the next boat show under last year's terms while we were asking how we would carve up the responsibilities and the cost of the show. They weren't giving us any answers, and while we could have played along and let them push us into retaking the financial responsibilities, we were worried. We ultimately had no other option but to tell them no. It was clear that they wanted to do things the way we did them the prior year, but we couldn't afford the risk and unfair split of the expense again.

This is where the real trouble began. No matter what we did, or how many times we pushed back and told them no, their answer was always the same, "You're just going to do this the way we've always done it."

At this point, my partner and I had to make a call. We decided that this had to be the end of the road for this manufacturer. The preexisting conditions were not sustainable. They were no longer a good match for the way we wanted to run our business, and they had left us with no other option.

After my dad's death, I had received a lot of advice from people telling me not to make any rash decisions while going through a major transition like losing a parent. People were constantly telling me that it is not a good time to be making decisions, but at this same point, I couldn't let this issue go. It had to be addressed, and we called a meeting and told our manufacturer, "Effective immediately, we resign as your dealer in the Midwest."

We had just fired a major manufacturer, *our manufacturer*, and we were left scrambling to figure out what comes next. You see, the interesting thing about this time was the way it seemed to set off a domino effect.

Previously unbeknownst to me, my business partner had his own desired outcome. So, when we made that call and we fired our manufacturer, the next thing I knew, he was trying to convince me to file bankruptcy. As it would turn out, he had managed to get himself into financial trouble, and he saw this as his way out.

I wasn't expecting this. I didn't see our situation in the same light he did. Also, my wife was working in financial services at the time, and I knew that had we filed for bankruptcy, the effect on not only my business, but my family, too, would have been numerable—just finding a job after that would have proved a challenge.

Not filing bankruptcy, though, caused its own set of trials. My business partner and I had been friends since high school. He was like a brother to me. We were so close we had even started our own business together. Now, that 15-year partnership seemed to dissipate in the blink of an eye.

It was difficult, but I would find out later that he was going through his own set of challenges with his family and his wife during this time. He had always struggled with balancing the expectations placed on him by his household and the business. He was a super hard worker and a family man, so the decision was challenging. There was a bit of upset there below the surface that spilled over into our business relationship. It hadn't been right for a while. So, beyond the crumbling of the business, our business relationship and friendship were falling apart also.

Their personal financial issues limited his options and eventually he decided to file bankruptcy. Our friendship was never the same after that. All of those steps, those transgressions, severed our relationship. I hadn't just lost a business partner the day he filed bankruptcy, but I lost a friend that I had known for 35 years. It ultimately strained our relationship. You could say it was the last straw.

So, there I was, down a manufacturer and a friend, and I had simply hit ground zero. At this point, I knew I had no other option than to survive, but I just kept asking myself how I had reached this point and, most of all, how could I survive...

CHAPTER 1:

A FOUNDATION BUILT ON FAMILY VALUES

"If you don't stick to your values when they are being tested, they're not values; they're hobbies."

~ Jon Stewart

So, where did that leave me? Back to the beginning, looking for the only explanation I could find to understand this new reality. How was I raised? What was the lesson of this experience? What would my dad advise me to do? "Man, I could really use my dad right now," I thought. I felt like life as I knew it was spiraling, and I had to stop the flat tailspin. I had to keep it together.

Growing up, it seemed like my family was always around. When mom and dad were not, an aunt, uncle, or grandparent was there, ready to fill in their shoes. It's typical for a Hispanic family to favor this extended structure. It's very ingrained in many of us from the beginning. I learned a lot in those early years about what it meant to be a family. Many of these lessons I still carry with me to this day with my own family. The values define who we are and how we operate.

My mom's family lived under one roof in my grandparents' house in South Chicago during my childhood. Because of my parent's work schedules, I would visit frequently, and their house would become the backdrop of my childhood. This three-bedroom house in Chicago was home to my uncles and aunts until they were married. And, growing up, they were always around.

One of my uncles, Uncle Frank, was an electrical engineer who worked for Ford Motor Company, and he would sometimes return home from work and take me on trips to the toy store for kits highlighting STEM projects–model kits and toys that would challenge me and allow me to build things with my hands. My other uncle, Oscar, worked for the railroad. Like many Hispanic men in underserved communities, they served in the military.

My Uncle Frank was in the Navy, and Uncle Oscar was in the Army. Neatly and proudly displayed on my grandparent's fireplace mantle were their pictures in their service uniforms. My Uncle Zeke Montes was another example of a community leader who served as a role model for his entire life. As a very public person, he showed me the importance of staying connected to the Hispanic community. As an entrepreneur and organizational leader, his lessons resonated with me.

As I grew, so did the lessons my uncles taught me. STEM projects turned to life lessons. They would impress on me the importance of using proper grammar and dressing neatly. They knew firsthand how tough the world could be for a Hispanic male–how the standards were different, and we needed to do everything our white counterparts did, and more. My uncles made sure I was presenting my best self to the world around me because they knew the challenges I would be facing.

My aunts had an impact on my life as well. They showed me the nurturing side of everything. They were very supportive in their approach. In those early years, both of my parents worked to give my four siblings and I the education they believed would make all the difference in our success. Plenty of sacrifices were made in those years, but because of the presence my extended family had in my life, I felt as though there was always someone there to support me when my mom and dad could not be.

MY MAN OF STEEL

I think most little boys have some sense of admiration for their father. I consider myself especially blessed in that category. My father, Trinidad Louis Sandoval, was the single greatest role model in my life. He was a quiet, unassuming man who kept a very low profile. On the flipside, when he did pipe up to say something, you knew that you had either really screwed up, or it was advice that you did not want to miss, especially as I got older. His humble upbringing, the way that he lived his life, and the values that he imparted upon us left an impression upon me like no other.

On my dad's side of the family, my grandfather worked in the Bracero program. It was a migrant worker program in the early twentieth century where migrant workers were given temporary work visas to come and work the fields of the United States. As farmers in their own country, this came naturally. My dad's entire family, a large one of six children, made their winter home in the town of Tanhuato de Guerrero in the state of Michoacán, a small town just outside of Morelia.

They lived in a small farmhouse that I was able to visit when I was very young. During the summers and harvest season, they would come to the plains states to work in the fields. This led to him and his younger siblings being born in cities like Des Moines, Iowa, Omaha, Nebraska, and Summit Lake, Minnesota, which is where my dad was born in 1930.

He would later tease during much of the controversy about illegal immigration that he and his siblings were the original anchor babies–born with American citizenship, an unintended consequence of the Bracero program. It was only natural that when his parents passed away in his teens, that he would act on his US citizenship and leave the small town in Mexico.

He traveled to Chicago to live with his older brother, Rafael, who had already established himself there and gained employment in the thriving industrialization of the Midwest states. Like many other Hispanics, who earned good money and raised their families working for companies like Republic Steel, Wisconsin Steel, and US Steel, my dad was hired by US Steel and began work at the age of eighteen.

Dad had the equivalent of an eighth-grade education because of all the mobility required in the Bracero program. Due to the economic necessity of having to work, he abandoned his desire to learn after taking some trade classes at Chicago Vocational High school on the Southside of Chicago and dedicated himself to reading, learning on the side, and working in the steel mill.

It was at US Steel where he worked for 41 years until pressure from the globalization of the steel industry and collision with organized labor interests caused the mills to close, evaporating over eighteen thousand jobs in the South Chicago area. Dad was part of this, and in 1992, with much life ahead of him, he was forced to retire early as US Steel Southworks closed its doors, never to open again.

My father's story taught me perseverance, commitment, love, and what a man was really responsible for–his family. There is a stereotypical characterization of the Latino male as a machista, hardworking individual who likes his women and his drinks. My dad was the furthest thing from that. He did not drink, was a family man, and put us front and center, sometimes to his own detriment.

FAMILY IS A TEAM

Mom and Dad embodied teamwork. They made a great team. My Mom, Bertha Sandoval, was born in Mexico City and is the oldest of six children. My grandfather on my mom's side came to Chicago in 1954. He started working at Republic Steel, and later brought grandmother, my mom, and her siblings to the states in 1956 once he was established.

Mom worked upon graduating from Bowen High School on the Southside. She was one of a few Hispanics at the school which was mostly composed of white, specifically Jewish, students that lived in the surrounding Jeffery Manor and South Shore communities prior to the white flight of the 60s and 70s. Mom and dad met in 1963 and got married in 1964.

Mom left her job to raise our family when my brother Martin was born in 1967. She took on different gigs at various times to supplement cashflow during tight times. I vividly remember one of them; the Tupperware sales period. Mom took on being a Tupperware sales lady, hosting gatherings for neighbors and family friends (and acquaintances) where the primary goal was to hustle the plasticware.

We would drive out in our family wagon to the Southwest side to pick up orders and later distribute them. In our family, she was the bank. You usually had to pitch your idea to her first, but she positioned dad as the ultimate decider. She was the gatekeeper, so we all learned the skilled art of pitching the gatekeeper whenever we wanted something. We got a lot of no's, but occasionally we would be successful.

I can only imagine the conversations between mom and dad, knowing some of the economic pressures of the times. I'm sure there were tensions due to finances. But if there were, my brother, sisters, and I did not know as mom and dad worked cohesively as a team. Dad would work, bring home the paycheck, and mom would backstop the household. In a world of two incomes and two working parents today, I really appreciate the impact that having my mom home had for me in my development. It created the comfort and stability that is so necessary to develop your confidence as a child.

TENACIOUS WORK ETHIC

At the mills, my father worked eight-hour shifts. There would be times when he was working for three to four days at a time. And then, if he got the opportunity, he would usually work a double shift because it was great to have more money coming in for him. With four mouths to feed, I am sure that was a huge motivator. After all, he was paid time and a half for working the second shift. With such a schedule, I might not see him for a few days at a time. Some weeks he would even work four days on, one day off, and then he'd go work the next shift.

Dad's work ethic was amazing. I remember a time when he serendipitously found out that he was allergic to strawberries. He wasn't a big believer in going to the doctor, and this was one of those instances. His body reacted to the strawberries by breaking out in hives and his eyes almost swollen shut. Dad was so committed to work (and supporting his family) that he went in that way. Most of us would have called in sick, but not pops. He played hurt-every time.

I remember times when my dad would work two or three shifts in a row, we would walk lunch over to the 83rd Street mill entrance, blocks from our house. It was some of the few times I would see dad in his work gear–hard hat, flame-resistant gear, steel toed boots, and dirt on his face where the goggles did not cover. My father would often say to my brother and I that he ate dirt and worked in his filth so we did not have to, so that we could be educated and make our living in a clean way.

I'm sure life was challenging for Dad given his commitment to family and needing to balance work and family life. While there were some things that made his life simpler, the lack of flexibility due to the constraints of his hourly job forced some decisions for him. This became more visible when I got a little older and started playing sports and getting involved with different things. He would have to place work above his presence to make ends meet.

He could never go to my little league games, my football games, or my hockey games. All of this because his schedule wouldn't allow him the time off. However, when he did get time off, he would prioritize that time and spend it with his family. Days when the whole family was free would become excursions. Time we would spend together as a family making memories. Whether we went to the Lincoln Park Zoo, the Field Museum, or even Grant Park, the goal was always the same–to spend time together as a family and extended family as grandparents, aunts, and uncles would be part of the excursions.

His dedication to providing for his family and spending time with us when he was able would continue throughout my childhood until the day his time working at the steel mill was suddenly over. He worked in the steel mill for a long 41 years, putting up with the harsh working conditions, an around-the-clock schedule, and the labor unions.

Ultimately, when things hit rock bottom in 1983, work became more unstable due to the labor union strife with the steel company. After almost a decade of instability, they closed the mills down in South Chicago in 1992. When they were done, they padlocked the door and just like that, 18,000 jobs went away. On a larger scale, my neighborhood on the South Side of Chicago never recovered from such a loss. Proud men and women lost their jobs, the labor organizers moved to Gary, Indiana, and Pennsylvania, and left a wake of rust, polluted land, broken dreams, broken homes, and the loss of dignity that comes with losing the ability to provide for your family.

This period of absence would continue and was felt in more ways than one in my own family. My father didn't give up working without resistance, but there was a whole period where he just wanted to go back to work. He had tuition to pay, a household to support, and it was extremely difficult on one bag of groceries a week, which is all his labor union seemed to offer.

My father was a very proud man. He wouldn't file for assistance and was ashamed to file unemployment. He believed wholeheartedly that these services were for those that needed them more than himself. He knew he still had the ability to work. He had to find a new way to support his family. My father still had a lot of work left in him, and he was determined to find a way to continue to support his family.

This was a tough time for him. All the work he had done his whole life was suddenly gone. Around-the-clock shifts turned into a constant search for odd jobs he could do to pay the bills. Through different neighborhood and career organizations that offered the displaced workers the opportunity for upskilling, dad took advantage of this by taking a GED course at the local city college to complete his high school diploma, once again fueling his passion for learning.

I now think back to all the stories of his years of hard work and recognize that they taught me so much about what it means to have perseverance. Why it is important to not give up, even when the odds are against you. Ultimately, these lessons influenced my desire to become an entrepreneur. In being an entrepreneur, I saw a bit more control over your destiny. I planned and pursued my passion because I had the perseverance he taught me.

BEING A PRESENT PARENT

Later in life–well into retirement–I remember asking dad once, in a period of silence, what he was thinking about, only to be shocked when he replied, "Thinking of all the things I could have done differently." I wasn't expecting this. I never expected him to regret the work he had done to support us growing up. Now looking back as a parent, I understand his desire to attend the school and sporting events for his children, but I hadn't expected him to admit to wanting to have been more present.

Looking back today, I recognized these sacrifices in the way I try to be present for my own family. In a way, my experiences growing up shaped who I would become not only as a father but as a business owner. In this way, the boat business was aspirational for me because it came along at just the right time. It allowed me to pursue a passion and turn a pastime into a living.

It came at a time when our daughters were small, so it gave me that flexibility. If I had to come in a half-hour later because I was dropping the girls off for school, helping with different activities in my daughter's classroom, when their classes put on performances, or there were sporting events, it was okay. It gave me the opportunity to be present.

When I look back at it, it's been a role in my life that I needed to happen. My wife always says that I got the best of the girls because I got to be there when they were young. And this is, without a doubt, true.

I can trace this opportunity all the way back to my childhood and the lessons I learned not only through my father's presence in my life but the priorities my whole family helped instill. The importance of supporting a family in all ways was there. My father made sacrifices so that I would not have to. He may have shown his commitment to family differently but, through his dedication to supporting us financially, the same fundamental idea is there. Family comes first.

This fundamental value would not be the only lesson he taught me. Through his years of hard work, I would also learn the importance of work ethic, something I would apply to my own work opening the boat dealership. He was one of the hardest workers I knew, and I continue to be proud of the sacrifices he made for our family to this day.

For me, dad served as the best role model I could ever ask for. I am proud to say now that I was the son of a steelworker who did more and achieved more to provide for his family in the best way he had available to him. He did so, at times sacrificing his own wants and dreams for those of his family. That commitment and his values have shaped me into who I am today.

CHAPTER 2:

IT'S ALL ABOUT FAMILY

"Don't let the world happen to you. You happen to the world." ~ **Ursula M. Burns**

To truly go back to the beginning, it becomes essential to look at the impact my grandmother had on my family. She was, after all, at the core of my family. So many of the lessons I gained through my father and extended family could all find their way back to her. She was a constant in my life and a steady guiding force for the entire clan. I believe that I got a lot of my grittiness from her. She was my foundation during the early years of my life, helping to raise me and teaching me many lessons along the way.

In the early years, my grandfather worked selling candy in a candy shop and was a tailor; my grandmother, on the other hand, was a schoolmarm for a boarding school in Mexico City. All six of her children attended the same boarding school where she worked. It was like a daycare in that sense. Because of my grandmother's job, she would spend her mornings getting all the children ready for school, and when the time came to leave, she would have to hustle them out in the morning and walk them to school.

My grandmother would shepherd them on their walk, almost as if she were a mother duck and her children her ducklings. In the evenings, once she was done at work, she would return home in a similar fashion. Because she had a family, she was lucky to be able to spend her evenings at home.

LEAVING MEXICO BEHIND

Unfortunately, with six children, she and my grandfather would struggle to make ends meet. This financially difficult time would lead them to consider their options and finally lead them to make the difficult decision to leave Mexico. Like many other immigrants, they decided to pursue the American dream in a new land. Immigration policy was a bit more stable in those days. You could find a sponsor (usually a family friend or relative in the States) and engage in the process to begin the naturalization process.

My grandfather got a traveler's visa and visited with friends in the states in 1954. He was drawn to Chicago because of the industrial development and good paying union jobs in the steel industry. My granddad had some family friends at the time who were already working at the Republic Steel mill on Chicago's far South Side, so my grandfather left first to find work, leaving my grandmother and their six children behind. My grandmother would later leave Mexico in 1956, two years after my grandfather with my mother and her siblings in tow.

Things didn't get easier right away when she came to the United States. With six children, paychecks still went faster than they were made, and there were many difficult times. Regardless, my grandmother always made sure to make the best of the difficulties she faced. As a side hustle, my grandad would make "Mexican candies," sweet treats that he would sell wholesale to neighborhood stores. I still remember the smell of caramelo, canela y azucar (caramel, cinnamon and sugar) in their kitchen. While it was a side hustle, it provided additional money to feed the family.

My grandparents were frugal, born in the depression era, they knew how to stretch a dollar. Even when it came to bootstrapping their own enterprise. My grandmother was probably the originator of that frugality. A simple proud woman, she was the backbone of the house and the matriarch of the family. She was an exquisite cook. Everything, and I mean everything, was made from scratch. Her signature dishes of mole verde (green mole sauce) have been passed down generations and her Mexican rice with peas were very popular (two of my favorite dishes to this day). Perhaps it was the time spent in the kitchen with both her and grandpa that influenced my knack for baking.

Aside from the traditional roles, grandma was very keen on being proper. Perhaps it was the school marm in her, but she was a stickler for no profanity, being a gentleman, and dignity. The many memories that she has left me with continue to guide me and lead me to understand what it takes to build a strong family foundation and apply the values that she contributed to my upbringing.

Her story and experiences have a very humbling presence in my life. Knowing what she experienced and where she came from has helped me try not to take things for granted, especially the time I have to devote to my own family.

NO FIGHTING ALLOWED

Though her lessons were wide-ranging, they always came back to our family. My grandmother was not a person that believed in violence. When my grandfather retired, their frugality paid off and they sold their Chicago home, pooled their savings, and moved to a suburb of Mexico City where they lived in a condo and would snowbird back and forth.

Growing up, I would spend time there and, at one point, I had made friends with all the kids in the neighborhood. I would ride skateboards, roller skate with them, play soccer, and all kinds of different things. One kid in the neighborhood was a bully because his dad owned a business, and he thought it provided him with a lot of privilege and that it made him a big shot, which led him to bully everybody at one point. On one specific occasion, I remember that we had been playing and, suddenly, he shoved me. I tried to walk it off, but then he went after my brother. When I told him to leave my brother alone, he threatened my grandmother (in a bit of a profane way). That was the last straw, and I went after him.

My grandmother had been watching from the fourth-floor apartment window. I remember her running down and pulling me out of the fight by the scruff. She says, "What are you doing? You're in trouble. We don't fight, we talk things out and make our point with our words. We don't use our hands." She started reprimanding me, asking me, "What were you thinking, fighting this kid," I said, Grandma, he said he was going to come after you, and then he called you a name." Then she said, "Pues mijo, dale," giving me the okay to finish the job.

Afterward, she took us upstairs, and she cleaned me up in the dining room. She took that opportunity to tell me that there are certain things that you must do. One of those things is to respect the honor and the dignity of your family. She never wanted to see me raise my hand to somebody; she advocated instead for working your way out of altercations with words. Instead of fighting, we were expected to use our brains.

In her words, "That is how you showed your education." But at the end of the day, if that's all you have left to do, to be physical with somebody, you must protect your family's honor. You need to teach people how to treat you and you should never allow someone to denigrate you or your family.

LESSONS OF PRIDE, HONOR, AND GOOD BEHAVIOR

I pondered on that time a lot, and I remember later in life talking to her about that incident, and I had asked her why she didn't want me to fight. She told me that it was because of my family's reputation and as a man of the house, what I did represented my family and could either honor them or shame them. She was a proud woman, and she believed in honor, even to the point of childhood fights.

Later in my life, I would be reminded of those early years and be conscious of how my actions affected not only me but my family. This would also be present in how she expected me to present myself to the world around me. When I was younger, my grandmother would often return to her boarding school days to tie in important lessons and make her points. One time that I remember were her lessons on presenting yourself in the best way you have available.

She would often tell us, "Listen, you can have one outfit to wear and be dirt poor. But it doesn't mean you have to be rude. It doesn't mean you have to be dirty. You have got to hold yourself to a higher standard." She would frequently tell stories of how kids at the boarding school would only have one outfit, their uniform. Each night they would wash it, they would dry it, and they would iron it the following day before they went to school. That's the type of standard that she held us to.

She also had a clear sense of needs and wants. Perhaps it was the depression era she grew up in, but it seemed to work for them. My grandmother had a very high sense of dignity, and she would make sure that you carried yourself in a dignified fashion as well. She would often have us iron our clothing if we were going to go anywhere in public. She wanted to make sure that you were presentable. Sunday mass was the same; when we went to masses, she did not accept going all sloppy. We had to wear a coat, a collared shirt, and, if possible, a tie. That was the beginning of understanding that I had to hold myself to a higher standard.

THE TRICKLE-DOWN EFFECT

These lessons would have a trickle-down effect and affect not only the way I dressed but also the way I communicated with the world around me. This was reinforced in the way she raised her sons. I had an uncle who ended up going into the Navy and another who served in the Army. Their Hispanic identity meant they had to work twice as hard at presenting themselves professionally. They were constantly telling me that there was only one way I would move up in my career, and that was learning how to explain myself clearly and how to speak without an accent.

My uncles' perseverance and almost overwhelming corrections of my language transferred much of what my grandmother believed. She had passed those same values to them, and then on to me. The slang and how I spoke mattered to them because they had learned, the same as I, that presentation matters and ultimately affects not only your reputation but that of your families. So, it was more of a continuation of values. You were expected to hold yourself to a higher standard and making sure that you didn't give the world a reason to judge you for being anything other than yourself.

As I made my career in the corporate world, I would often remember those lessons. To this day, I've learned that it is one thing to make it and be included, but there is a different expectation put on you as a Hispanic, bi-cultural person. You don't get the same privilege that others get. At times it seems like the world expects you to fail–it has low expectations because of the stereotypes and biases that are perpetuated. If we fail, it's almost proof that they were validated in their thoughts. With so few like us in corporate America, we have few mentors who look like us and perhaps relate to us.

So, we are judged differently. I think learning those things from my family and my grandmother helped me later in life. My grandmother drilled into us the value of taking the time, in any experience, to present yourself in a way that shows respect to those you surround yourself with.

SELF-ADVOCATING FAIR TREATMENT

This idea of presenting oneself also led my grandmother to stress the importance of being treated fairly by others. Being a self-advocate was essential.

Before they moved, I would go to the grocery store with my grandmother. She used to buy groceries with special coupons that could be traded in for money, S&H Green Stamp books. On one occasion, she had two books that she had saved that could be traded in for $10. However, because she didn't speak the best English, the man at the checkout tried to convince her that the two books she had saved were only worth $5. This made my grandmother very angry. She threw the booklets on the counter, and she told him in English, as best she could, that he needed to give her the $10 credit, not $5.

If he thought that he could take advantage of her because she didn't speak English, this was not the case. She even threatened to start yelling at the top of her lungs until she got the attention of somebody that would give her the full $10. The manager eventually got involved, and he ended up giving her the full $10. This event taught me a lot about not only the way presentation matters, but the actions behind it do as well. You must be ready to know your worth and show it to the world around you. On that day, all those years ago, she reminded me that you should never let anybody give you less than you're due to receive, ever.

A STRONG FAMILY UNIT

Grandma was a force to be reckoned with, but a force that taught me so much about what it means to live with pride and dedication to one's family. I see her presence constantly in my actions and the actions of my daughters.

In my nuclear family, and as the oldest child of four, I also took on the responsibility of shepherding my siblings in my own way. My brother Martin and I shared a room for most of our youth. This made for some interesting adolescent boy things—like pounding on each other, but having to make up when it was all over. Sibling stuff, but through all of that— even when we lived on opposite corners of the country, him in Boston and me in Seattle we were always there for each other. He always has been, and always will be, my ride or die.

My sisters Susana and Anabel shared their own room, too. The six and nine-year age difference probably impacted their perspective of me as I was in high school and then out of the house during their tween and teen years. When I lived away from Chicago, I made it a point to try and be the uncle that my uncles were to me—to my nephews and nieces.

In the same way we learned, the next generation was shown that a "simple family gathering" in Latino fashion is sixteen plus people (now that we factor in nieces and nephews and significant others). Sonia and I have proudly hosted Thanksgiving at our house almost every year since we were married (save a distant Thanksgiving during the pandemic). There is no simple way to do family—at my house it is a full contact, major event.

Though she is now gone, my grandma's lessons, and that sense of family which came down from her and was reinforced by my mom and dad, continue to live on in our own families.

CHAPTER 3:

GROWING UP PLAID

"Don't let what you cannot do interfere with what you can do." ~John Wooden

My grandmother didn't just talk about the importance of family, she lived by example and had a huge influence on my life.

Some kids might complain if their parents' job took them away as much as my parents did in my early years, but not me. Being raised by my grandparents was a blessing, and I thrived there. I relished the afternoons at her house asking her about what it was like being a little girl in Mexico. She would tell me about how tough it was for her.

Her father made it very tough on her growing up, much of which came from a lack of respect for women, but also due to the cultural norms of the era in which she grew up. The predominant mindset was that men ran the house and women were to be subservient. One of the beautiful things about Mexico is the culture, and one of the not-so-great facts is that the culture is pretty misogynistic. Machismo still prevails, and women don't have a fair say. Things are changing, but as a father of two daughters, not fast enough for my tastes.

My grandmother had been an educator at a boarding school in Mexico prior to moving to the US, and she insisted on proper Spanish, proper diction, no slang words, and holding yourself to a higher standard. Thanks to her, I became fluent in Spanish, and I'm indebted to her for a lot of the lessons that I received throughout my life. She occasionally visits me in my dreams, usually when I'm at a crossroads in decision-making, so I know she is near. My abuelita would teach me through "los cuentos de la abuelita regañona" (the stories from grumpy grandma), stories that I wish I had recorded, because as the years go on, they fade.

Like most kids, memories from my early years are scattered and a bit foggy, but I remember my first day of kindergarten as though it was yesterday.

I was so excited to start school. I had been taken to the store to choose my lunch box, a hard metal box with a thermos inside and my favorite cartoon, Scooby-Doo, painted on the outside.

The big day came. It was the first day of school and we were waiting outside. I was so excited. One kid came up to me and asked, "What's your name?" I responded in

Spanish, so he looked at me kind of oddly, walked away, and didn't talk to me anymore.

We went into the classroom and I was one of those nerdy kids that likes sitting right in front of the teacher all the time. We all sat down on the floor, criss-cross applesauce, right in front of the teacher.

During recess that first week, I tried to play with some of the kids, but they shunned me because I didn't understand or speak English. Eventually, I grabbed a ball and started kicking it against the wall while everyone else was playing tag or some other activity in the main part of the playground.

NO CUTTING IN LINE

When it was time to go in, we all lined up single file and I was first in line. It had rained the day before and there was a puddle nearby, but I didn't notice at first. Up beside me came the kid who had asked my name on the first day, and he tried to cut in front of me.

Well, you know there is no cutting in line. I was trying to communicate that point in English but obviously it came out in Spanish, and as he pushed me out of the way, I lost my balance and fell. I landed in the puddle sideways and got all muddy. All the other kids in line started laughing, and he said, "Speak English so we can understand you."

I was pissed off, but my mom and grandmother would always tell me not to get in fights, so I held back, went into class, and asked my teacher if I could go to the bathroom. I wiped myself down with paper towels, but I was a muddy mess.

Our house was just around the corner from the school, so when we were let out of the classroom after the day was over, I ran all the way home. I was still mad and embarrassed. I went in the back door, ran downstairs, and took all my clothes off.

I was running upstairs in my underwear when my mom stopped me to ask, "What happened to you?" I told her what happened and explained that the boy didn't understand me and that all the kids had laughed at me

That night at dinner, my dad said, "Listen, you know, you're going to have to learn to adjust to the environment and speak English, so you'll be able to communicate. They're obviously not going to understand Spanish."

So, the next day I was very quiet and reserved. I'm did not want to sit in the front of the classroom. Instead, I sat in the back of the room, embarrassed. For that whole week I hid out in the classroom, avoiding contact with anyone and kept to myself.

LEARNING ENGLISH VIA SESAME STREET

It wasn't long before I decided to do what my dad said. I would come home every day after school and watch Sesame Street. It was Ernie, Bert, Big Bird, Mr. Roper, and the team that basically taught me English, because in watching the show, I was listening to it, and I would repeat the words that they would say.

In my mind it was only a week before I was speaking English, but it was probably longer than that. Those times when they would speak in Spanish and then in English helped accelerate my learning curve.

After that, I was able to go in. And I remember, once I felt comfortable being able to communicate, going up to that kid and telling him, "I can speak English now. I don't ever want you to push me again, because if you push me, I'm going to have to do something that I don't want to do."

I wasn't pushed or ridiculed, but it started to shape my perception that standing out was not the way to be, I needed to fit in, blend, and be more accultured.

TRYING TO FIT IN

That experience makes me think of how it must've been for my mom when she came to the United States at the age of 14, in 1956. She was already pretty far along in her education, but they put her in the sixth grade because she didn't understand English.

Back then there was no such thing as English as a Second Language (ESL). She would have been in her freshman year of high school at that point. Can you imagine the humiliation of that?

My whole experience with that kid, just like it was for my mom at 14, was the first time when I realized I was different from the other kids. You don't think you are while you're in the process of growing up but as I compared myself later in life to my mom, I thought about what it must have been like for her.

Holding true to the adage that kids are resilient, eventually, mom was able to test out of sixth grade. They then put her into eighth grade with her younger brother, who was 12, and they ended up graduating high school together.

For my mom and her generation, it was about trying to fit in. Diversity wasn't a thing that people embraced back then. It was more an attitude of how can you keep your head down, blend in, and get the job done as opposed to how do you stand out? As I found out that first day of kindergarten, things had not changed much fifteen years later.

For most of my life, I was raised with the kindergarten experience—the differences that divided us versus those that make us more powerful. As we have sought out schools to educate our daughters, we've settled on schools with an emphasis on diversity. In much of what we have learned during the pandemic, these issues are still critical for underrepresented communities.

OUR NEIGHBORHOOD

When I was in first grade, we were living in the Cottage Grove Heights neighborhood in Chicago. We lived at 9735 S. Dobson through 7th grade and moved to the South Chicago community that summer. In grammar school, in the Burnside neighborhood at 92nd and Kimbark Avenue, I was one of two or three Hispanic kids in the class. Three-quarters of the school was white and the rest mostly African American. It was a pretty diverse group by older standards.

The Burnside neighborhood was historically Hungarian, with a lot of Hungarian immigrants there who built the parish, Our Lady of Hungary, and then a school above the parish. Like many communities in Chicago, their parish was emblematic and a safe space for their community.

At the point when I was going to Our Lady of Hungary, it was in transition and "white flight" happened, when everyone pulled out and went to the suburbs or other areas and they were replaced by strong, middle-class African American families.

The neat thing about that is we all had the common theme of wanting to better ourselves through education. This area was on the far South Side of Chicago, and it was vastly different from other areas of the city. You had the steel mills, a lot of industry, and good paying middle-class jobs. My dad worked as a steelworker for 41 years and he was able to put four kids through private Catholic schools, including a Catholic high school. That's the foundation that allowed us to get scholarships, to go to college, and then grad school and all that great stuff. That was the core of what Chicago was back in the 70s and 80s.

As the school started to kind of change in about third grade, it started to become predominantly African American, and I was now one of two or three lighter skinned people in the class. So, once again I was different because I wasn't in one camp. I'm not white and I'm not black. I'm kind of in the middle, and, ironically, most Catholic schools used a uniform. Ours were brown. The boys wore brown pants and an ecru shirt with a plaid tie, and the girls wore a plaid brown skirt, a pattern that mapped our path.

As I look back on it, the, that pattern was emblematic of how I grew up. I didn't quite belong in the white part of the crosshatch pattern, and I didn't fit into the black part, either. I was the brown part of it—growing up plaid.

I grew up listening to music from the O'Jays, Earth, Wind and Fire, R&B, and soul music. I was also learning what the Black National Anthem, "Lift Every Voice and Sing," was because some of our teachers were African American. They would sing the spiritual that gave them hope during the Jim Crow and slavery era. I learned a lot about the black culture and how they had to overcome adversity, and I also had a lot of very close black friends.

All around us, families were part of the working middle class with common goals of education and most of us went to Catholic grammar school, Catholic high school because they believed private schools were better than Chicago Public Schools.

There wasn't the vibrancy that there is today when you go to Pilsen. South Chicago was a melting pot for everybody whose parents worked at the steel mill. There was a little bit of everything—you had a Polish parish in the neighborhood, and a Hispanic parish, Our Lady of Guadalupe, where we went to church. I was in seventh grade when we moved from the Burnside neighborhood and switched to St. Michael the Archangel.

So, once again I was different. Throughout grammar school I had this understanding that I really didn't—couldn't—fit in. I could try to embrace the black culture, but

I didn't fit in because, ultimately, if you liked a girl, she might not like you back because you didn't look like her. They'd say, "You're white, you know?" And I would say, I'm not white and I'm not black. I'm Hispanic. That didn't change things, so again, there was that common theme of being different. Again, it was that theme of I can't be like them because I'm not. I can embrace it, but that doesn't matter—it is what it is.

THE WRATH OF SISTER BERTHA

I was always a good student and usually in the top three of my class. In fifth grade we had a teacher, Sister Bertha. She was a very tough, Hungarian lady with big chubby arms, and when you saw Sister Bertha, "the penguin," coming, you would duck. She was all about corporal punishment and she was extremely rough on the boys.

This year she had come to school with a Six Flags souvenir. It was an oar shaped like a large paddle that she called The Equalizer. She took that out of the first week of school and said, "If you don't behave..." It took her about a week and a half before she broke it on one of the kids' backs.

She literally broke the paddle on him. Her wind-ups would put Hank Aaron to shame, and I remember the day the paddle broke because I was in one of the rows towards the front. The splinters flew all over the place, and we all looked at each other in disbelief.

She was brutal. I got caught one time playing flip with the girls' skirts. The boys would do it to see what color underwear they had on. You know, things that you probably shouldn't be doing. And I tell my daughters that it's the stupid boy way of showing they probably have a crush on you, but they don't know how to deal with it.

So, that day three of us got caught playing flip. She put us in front of the whole class, put two pencils on the floor for each of us, and we had to kneel on the pencils while holding a dictionary in each hand with our arms stretched all the way out to the side. You had to hold them for as long as she said. It was basically a crucifixion in front of the class. If you dropped one, she would whack you on your behind with two wooden rulers.

I never went home with any of this to my parents. My dad would always say, "If I get called into school because of something you're doing, I'm going to listen to what you did and then you're going to get a double punishment at home."

The next year, in sixth grade, I had a great teacher, Ms. Hoffman. I flourished in sixth grade under her because she was positive and reaffirming and taught us a lot. It was a bit of positive therapy after being brutalized in fifth grade. Ms. Hoffman came along at a critical time for me. I don't think any of us could take another year like fifth grade.

As seventh grade came around, I had another teacher, Ms. Packard who was mean and she would beat kids, too, just like the nuns. She was a plainclothes teacher, and she was what they call a lay teacher. We used to think that Ms. Packard was much like the tender at the sharecropper's farm who was in charge of whipping the slaves. Not that we were slaves, but she sure seemed to derive pleasure from the brutalization of her students. I'm sure we were a tough bunch at times, but it was a different time when education was punctuated by the beatings we would receive.

As I think back on that time, it is hard to believe that my parents actually spent their hard-earned money for us to be beat. None of this would be legal today. My daughters can't fathom that any of this could happen as their world is very different, thank God.

GRANDMA ALWAYS SAID...

Then came eighth grade and, unfortunately, I got Sister Bertha again. We'd had a rough year because she was at the end of her career and losing her sanity.

She would constantly egg us on with negative talk and create a self-fulfilling prophecy by saying, "You guys are all bad kids, very bad kids."

When we were in seventh grade, the eighth graders went to Washington, D.C., and two of them must have hooked up because one of the girls got knocked up. So, the next year, when we would have gone, they canceled the trip and fired the teacher. I guess we can thank the class of 1978 for the fact that we got Sister Bertha.

At one point in the school year, and this was towards the end because I remember it was hot that day and we'd just come in from recess.

Sister Bertha was trying to keep us quiet because kids in eighth grade check out the last half of the year. You're just ready for graduation, to be done with the whole thing. So, she had us put our heads down and be quiet. That was her way of controlling us, and if we were doing something, she would hit people.

There was a girl that was next to me, Kim Pass. We were talking across the aisle and suddenly I looked over, and out of the corner of my eye I saw Sister Bertha coming fast with her arm winding up, and I knew she's about to hit me.

That's when I heard my grandma's voice saying, "You got to teach people how to treat you. You can't let anybody do anything to you." My next thought was, "Yeah, but this is a frigging nun and I'm going to go to hell."

Just as she's about to swing at me, I put my arm up to block the shot. But as I do, she was still in her wind up and her arm hit mine. I blocked the shot but as I moved away, I caught the back of her helmet, as we called it. Technically, it's called a habit.

I knocked her helmet off by accident. Imagine this stout lady, with gray hair, glasses and a soup bowl haircut (sort of an olden days, gray Dora the Explorer haircut) Her habit hits the ground and it just sat there for a moment in what seemed like an eternity. She looked super funny in front of the whole class. Then she roared and as she tried to come at me a second time with her second shot, I got up and ran to the front of the classroom.

I was not going to let her hit me. I had gotten fed up with

the fact that she had beat us, abused us, and did all these things to us. The class was in an uproar, and I walked out into the hallway.

Two other teachers showed up because they could hear the commotion and Sister Bertha, screeching at the top of her lungs with her strong Hungarian accent, "You're going to go to hell!"

Then, along came the principal whose office was right next to our classroom. Sister Celeste was a very tight looking lady with dark hair, and horn-rimmed glasses. She came over and told me to go to her office. After she talked to Sister Bertha in nun code—or however they communicated—she then asked me what happened. She said, "I'm going to send you home right now. We're going to call your mother and tomorrow you're going to need to come in with both your mother and your father or you will not be allowed back at school."

Now comes the most challenging part. I had to tell my parents what had happened since I'd been sent home. My mom was shocked. I had to wait for my dad that evening because my dad always worked shifts. When he had a day shift, as he did that day, he didn't get home until six or seven o'clock.

I was sweating it out, waiting for the conversation with my dad. My dad couldn't just call off work and say, "I'm going to go in and deal with my delinquent son's problems at school." So, my mom goes into school the next day and everybody's like, Lou is going to get kicked out of school.

The moment of truth came, the visit with mom to the principal's office. They said they wanted me to write an apology letter to Sister Bertha and they would get it to her. She had a nervous breakdown or something at that point because we never saw her ever again, and we got a substitute teacher for the remainder of the year.

Sister Celeste said to my mom, "We treated him like one of ours and he failed." My mom asked what she meant by that and was told they didn't treat me like the rest of the kids, like the black kids. They treated me like one of them (the white staff) and, apparently, I let them down. That really stung with my mom because it was straight out racism. I guess they thought I deserved some sort of special privilege and I shouldn't be treated like the black kids (although I was).

Once again, I was stuck in the intersection between the plaids.

They let me graduate and didn't strip me of my salutatorian honors. In fact, I think I got more of a round of applause when I gave my speech on graduation day, but as we finished the school year out, I ended up graduating number two in the class. It was rumored that they knocked me down a notch, but my guess is that those antics cost me the number one spot.

At that point, our family had already moved to south Chicago to be closer to my dad's job. So, cutting ties with Our Lady of Hungary was ok. I was transitioning to high school and that was that.

I have some very rich friendships that I made back in

Grammar school, and I still keep tabs with a few of my friends. I remember, many of us went on to attend Catholic high schools—Mendel, Mt. Carmel, Leo, St. Francis, Mother Seton–because all the families were focused on giving the next generation the next leg up.

We all went on to attend some great universities, too– Northwestern, DePaul, Loyola, Howard. Many from that Cottage Grove Heights neighborhood went on to become judges, business owners, entrepreneurs, and nurses. It was our fulfillment of the American dream. It seems to me this is when the South Side was at its height and we were proud south siders full of grit, perseverance, and the hunger to move ahead in the world.

INVITED TO CUB SCOUTS

In fourth grade, a parent came to our classroom and gave a presentation on Boy Scouts. There was a troop at our school, he said and then asked us, "Wouldn't you like to be a part of it?"

I went ahead and joined and when I moved to the new neighborhood in seventh grade, I transferred troops to the one at St. Michaels.

Scouting was a safe space for me because scouting allowed me to be different. I was really into science and that made me different in itself. So, going into scouting allowed me to explore my interest in science even more because of the merit badges and all the different things that we did. And that was the one area where, maybe because of the uniform and the fact that we all had common interests it was a safe space and I felt comfortable there. I could be the nerdy science kid if I wanted to be.

It felt kind of like my superpower. That and baseball gave me a sense of normalcy. I was a huge baseball nut as a kid. I liked to go to baseball games. I collected baseball cards, and I did box scores with my grandfather at Cubs games and I attended Sox games with my dad at the old Comiskey Park.

Scouting helped me as I was trying to find my identity in a world that kept shutting me out and making me feel like I didn't really belong anywhere. While passionate about math and science, I had to work extra hard. I needed tutoring in grammar school and later high school to be able to master Algebra. Mom did what she could early on, but as the material got tougher, we had to reach for outside help from tutors and neighbors.

I think at times, my mom would grow frustrated with my challenges in math. Perhaps she thought I was lazy or just didn't apply myself. Those feelings would eat into my self confidence in math. I would freeze at the chalkboard in HS algebra when my teacher would ask me to come up front to solve problems. The numbers would jumble for me and I did not know why. I started to believe that was just the way I was made–perhaps dumb. I had to try extra hard to get good grades.

Scouting allowed me to overcome that and be part of something that was important to me. It rebuilt my self-esteem and allowed me to apply math to the world around me in ways that made sense to my brain.

MY SUPERPOWER

Many years later, while still a freshman in college at DePaul, I was coming out of psychology class and saw an advertisement during one of my gap periods for a graduate study test. "Earn fifty dollars" it said. Curious, and needing the money, I attended. It was then that I would find out that I had a mild form of dyslexia. More importantly, I was referred to a clinician at the student health department that helped me with exercises to concentrate and focus. I learned "Lou tricks" some of which I still use to this day to keep numbers on profit and loss statements clear so that they do not become jumbled.

I also use tricks with a teleprompter in speeches. It has been my superpower that I have often kept hidden from colleagues for fear that I might be judged, and from supervisors for fear that it might mean I don't get a promotion. From many circles, I feared that my differences may be seen as a deficiency or weakness. That I be pitied or, worse yet, ridiculed.

I have read much on the subject of dyslexia in the works of Dr. Sally E. Shaywitz, M.D from Yale's center on Dyslexia. To my surprise, there are some very famous and successful people who have dyslexia that have turned it into a superpower. Individuals such as classic wunderkind-Winston Churchill, Carl Jung, Albert Einstein and Leonardo Da Vinci.

On a global business level Sir Richard Branson, Charles Schwab, and even Shark Tank's Mr. Wonderful, Kevin O'Leary, and business magnate and yachtsman, Ted Turner. More locally, successful businesswoman and economist– Diane Swonk. All individuals that we would not think to be blessed with dyslexia. Conversely, individuals who have left an amazing imprint in our world. Expanding my knowledge on famous dyslexics has given me the power to know that I am not broken, I am not dumb–I'm just different. It has allowed me to embrace my difference as a superpower and as a compliment to my other strengths.

I fully understand and I am profoundly grateful for the differences that I have been blessed with. The Rich tapestry of my childhood experiences has fundamentally molded me into the person that overcomes obstacles and the person that turns those obstacles into advantages. It is in this plaid tapestry that I have found my strengths, my superpowers.

We all have the capacity to do this. We are all born with the capability to persevere and achieve. To do this, it is incumbent upon us to seek the support, the knowledge, that we need to turn our negatives into positives and to *wear our plaid proudly.*

CHAPTER 4:

THE INVITATION

---

*"A thought, even a possibility, can shatter and transform us." ~ **Friedrich Wilhelm Nietzsche***

Much can happen to us when we feel included. The sense of possibility becomes reality. It can be transformative. For a silly little boy from the South Side with a penchant desire to understand what made things 'click,' being a Boy Scout offered that possibility for me.

Scouts gave me a place to fit in at a time when I did not always feel that I did. As I think about how I got started, the opportunity for scouting happened when there was a scouting trip at our grammar school, and they hosted a meeting in the parish basement at Our Lady of Hungary, the first grammar school that I went to and graduated from.

It was in the Burnside neighborhood, and the neat thing about that community was that it was a mix of Hungarian,

African American, and a little bit of everything else. I was in fifth grade when I was approached by a couple of parents who had their kids in Cub Scouts.

They asked me to come to one of their meetings, but I was not sure since I had never been involved in Boy Scouts before. They explained how easy it was and how little it cost to join—about three dollars for annual dues and five cents in troop dues per week.

I asked my parents if it would be okay and told them I had money in my piggy bank to pay for it, so they gave me permission, and then I discovered I needed a uniform, which would cost more money. I was able to talk my parents into buying me the shirt and the neckerchief, which I also needed. It was a compromise, because as I was clearly aware, there were others to feed at home. I made do without the full pants. I spoke to the scoutmaster about this and he agreed to let me use cleanly pressed pants and as soon as a set of hand-me downs became available in my size, he would work on getting them to me.

Scouting was neat because we did a lot of arts and crafts, and I got to meet a new set of kids. Some of the kids went to my school, and some of the kids lived in the neighborhood and went to other schools. This exploration allowed me to continue to develop. When I think back to these days, I am very thankful that this opportunity presented itself. It was transformational for me, and came along at the right time.

A CURIOUS KID

For all the kids in our Scout Troop #1750 from Our Lady of Hungary, our common theme and bond was that we all had that passion for being outdoors, and I was already a little kid who was curious. I loved to play in the prairie, collect tadpoles, frogs, and snakes and keep them as pets. I loved to walk in the woods and would relish every opportunity to walk through a prairie adjacent to our block in my early home on Dobson Street.

When I was younger, I had a couple of goldfish. I was always interested in what was inside the goldfish, and then the day eventually came when our goldfish died. One of my uncles had given me a science kit with a microscope, a scalpel, and some other dissection tools. I decided that I was going to take some of the scales off the goldfish and look at them under the microscope.

Then I decided that I was going to cut it open because I wanted to see what it looked like inside. I remember thinking, "Oh, that's kind of neat. It's got guts." When I was done, I wrapped it in a napkin and buried it in the backyard, where we buried the rest of my pets as they died.

I have always been interested in nature and would collect tadpoles from a nearby pond and watch them mature into frogs. I would do the same thing with snakes, bring them in, and raise them until they got bigger.

We got a few kids from my class who also joined the troop. The nice thing about Scouts is that while there was a big push on science and learning through merit badges, it helped me with my curiosity to know what made things "tick" beyond the science that we covered in school. It gave me a platform to investigate and learn more about the things that interested me at the time, it was what most likely generated my desire to become a doctor early on in my educational endeavors.

SOGGY CAMPOUT

We would go to the spring Camporee every year at Hoover scout camp in Yorkville, which is about fifty miles west of Chicago. It was right on the Fox River and was an amazing place, but it always seemed to rain like crazy. Every time we went to the spring Camporee at Hoover, there was a torrential downpour.

For a kid from the city, it seemed like it took forever to get there. We would leave right after school, and we had to meet at the scout master's house with our pack and our sleeping bag. They put everything in the back of the scout master's station wagon, and we all jumped into one or two cars, and drove out there.

It was always night by the time we would get there, so we would be pitching tents in the dark, under the headlights of the car, which was an experience. The first time we did it, we had never pitched a tent before. We did not know what the things looked like, and we were working from the older Scouts' and Scout Master's descriptions of what has to go where, and it was a hot mess. And, if that was not enough, the sky opened, and it began to rain. I mean it rained buckets.

Here we are pitching tents in the rain, and we decided, all right, let us get one up, put all our gear inside of it, and then put get up another one. So, we pitched two tents—large tents—and we five in one in five and another. It was a miserable experience, but at the same time, kind of fun because the next day, we took stuff out and dried it on a clothesline over a fire. Some of the kids did not fare so well. They started crying—they did not like it and wanted to go home.

That kind of thing usually makes or breaks your experience, but for me, it was fascinating. One, you got a chance to sleep outside. Two, the campfires, and three, going down to the river and fishing. That was amazing for me. I loved it, and I loved being in the outdoors. Despite the horrible experience of the pitching of the tents in the rain, I was drawn to it. Some of my friends did not hang in there as much, and a couple of my good friends dropped out.

I stuck it out, gained my merit badges, and when I moved in eighth grade and transferred to another troop, I had a lot of my advancement requirements done. I went from Troop 2750 to 1750 to 750. The new troop was very active. They were in a church, and they had their own room in the rectory basement.

SUMMER CAMP IN MICHIGAN

My new troop was in South Chicago, where we had moved when I was in seventh grade to be closer to my dad's work. Our troop was meeting at St. Michael's the

Archangel, which is the parish three blocks from my house. This was the summer after seventh grade, and I had never gone to summer camp with my previous troop. Everyone said you have to come try this because you haven't lived until you've gone to summer camp.

We went for two weeks, and it was a tough conversation, getting my parents to allow me to leave for two weeks to a sleepaway camp. Being fairly tight knit, this is a big deal in the Hispanic community. After a lot of begging and pleading, I got my parents to say it was okay, and we had to sell candy to raise money to go.

My dad helped me sell candy at work, and we did all this stuff to raise the money so I could go to camp. When I think back to it, it was relatively inexpensive. However, for a working-class family with four kids in parochial/private schools, we all vie for financial resources and the ups and downs of the steel mills made it tougher on disposable income.

The very first Summer that I went to Scout camp at Owassippe, I heeded the advice everybody gave you, to maximize all your outdoor merit badges because those are the ones you will not get a chance to do in the winter.

Now was the time to do the outdoor ones–pioneering, swimming, archery, rifle, all that stuff. We did all of that. As I went through my list, I signed up for orienteering and canoeing. I signed up for all the ones that I had to do, and then I am like— all right! —there is a sailing one. I had never done it, but I had always loved the water, so I wanted to give it a shot.

When it was time, I went to the sailing outpost, which was over at Big Blue Lake, and I did not know anything about sailing. They start you with the nomenclature of the boat—what is a sheet, guy, mast, sail, hall, port, starboard—all the great things that you need to know about the boat. Then, on day two I went out sailing. I did not know how to catch the wind in the sails, and the instructor was getting impatient with me when I finally got it.

One of the things that I liked was the ability to get away from the shore and go out on the lake on this little sailboat. And I remember what really captivated me was the sunset over the lake, as it was starting to get dusky, and I was supposed to bring the boat back.

I did a waggle, moving the rudder to get the boat moving again because it was a light boat. There was a light breeze, and I remember putting the boat away and just sitting on the beach, watching the sun go down over the water. To this day, one of the best things I like to watch are sunsets over the water. For me, that captured the sense of exploration, of being able to get away from the shore, to be free on the water, and it became a passion.

The next summer, after eighth grade, I went back and took another sailing class. I loved that the experience was so liberating. After my summers at camp, I didn't get a chance to sail much. In high school, I focused on other sports. I stuck with scouting through the completion of my rank requirements to obtain Eagle, but I never got a chance to sail again. The teaser was that my childhood house is literally two-and-a-half blocks from the lake. Since we were working class, there was no club where we could join (or at least none that I knew of), so getting out sailing was limited to Scouting. I put my passion on mothballs when I went to high school and college.

SAILING, MY OLD "FRIEND"

Little did I know that later in life, when I was working, some of my colleagues would ask if I wanted to go sailing J24's out of Waukegan Harbor.

I told them that I had not sailed since I was a kid, but I would try it. So, I started crewing on Thursday nights, and I used it as an opportunity to meet my colleagues and build comradery. It served a purpose, and then, later on, my career took me to Seattle, and that's where I joined a yacht club, Seattle Caribbean, to continue sailing J24s.

I did not know anybody, so it was a great opportunity to meet people. I went, and I started sailing on Wednesday nights, sailing with everybody there, and before you know it, I am doing regattas and it was a lot of fun. I started meeting people, and I was already involved in the community. Then, I started talking to customers–these are all physicians, surgeons, and the like, and I noticed some of them had boat artifacts in their office–pictures, compasses, and barometers mounted on their walls.

I took that opportunity to strike up a conversation about boating, and they would almost always say it was sitting in the harbor. As this went on, I would hear the same response time and again. I decided to create a business to meet this apparent need since I was already immersed in the marine community.

MY FIRST MARINE VENTURE

Inside my boating circles, I started talking to a diesel technician, an electronics guy, and a guy that did boat washing and cleaning. I told them I would run all my business through them—I would manage it and bring in the clients. So, I pitched the boat owners and said, listen, if we could have somebody that could take care of your boat, maintain it, supply a crew, and have it ready to go if you wanted to just ride and entertain your clients, would it be worth X dollars a month?

I would price the concierge service based on the size of the boat and I ran it as a side hustle. They gave me the trust of using their vessel.

I also did a couple of races. One of my clients wanted to do the Vic Maui, so we worked out the logistics to get the boat on a truck all the way to Victoria, British Columbia, Canada. We got the boat up to Victoria, and then we left on the Vic Maui race from Victoria all the way across the Pacific to Hawaii.

Then, another guy wanted to do the transpacific race. We managed the logistics of getting a captain to bring his boat all the way down to Los Angeles and left from there. I did the race with him twice, across the Pacific from LA to Honolulu, and then another guy asked if we would go from Newport Beach California to Ensenada, Mexico.

It was amazing that the kid who first sailed on that little lake in Michigan now had a chance to see the sunsets in the Pacific as he sailed under the light of the moon, going through the Tradewinds. You are basically getting pushed along, and you wear nothing but shorts because it's so darn warm out, but there's enough breeze to have the boat moving at 17-18 knots.

It was phenomenal, and it was also an escape. I worked out the vacations with my real job so that I could be gone when I needed to be and also have time to coordinate and get things ready. It served the purpose of helping me be a good organizer of things and satisfied my sense of adventure.

From a career perspective, it allowed me to unfold my passion for science and everything that had to do with science, physics, and even math, what today people call STEM. It created a foundation for me, and it all started with an invitation.

If that had not happened, I would not have had the chance to sail in the race from Chicago to Mackinac Island once, much less twenty-one times and winning it nine times. It shows the possibility of what your life can become when somebody creates that spark for you through a simple invitation.

You never know the significance that opening might have in someone's life, foundationally or otherwise. There is a saying in pioneering that the pioneer's job is to go where no one has gone and to leave a trail, so others will follow. I think my entree into scouting was that way of creating a path for other stuff to follow.

DREAMING OF THE FUTURE

My dream is to someday create a foundation that would allow that skill to be shared with kids from underserved communities so that they can get out on the water and explore, because sailing teaches you a lot of amazing things.

I tell my daughters every day when I drop them off at sailing camp that it teaches you how to organize your life in a systematic way. It also teaches you how to be resilient because once you are out on the water and you have left the shore, you have to adjust and deal with whatever comes at you.

Obviously, this pandemic has shown everybody how resilient we can be when we are faced with challenges. A sailor's mindset teaches us how to dictate our outcome. For me, that invitation was foundational and put everything in perspective.

As I look back on it, I see how I had to go down that path. It has become my mindset in life—to stick with the course and see it through. Becoming an Eagle Scout opened a lot of doors for me, especially when interviewing for college and jobs later in life. When people find out you are an Eagle Scout, it is a different level, a sort of entry card to a special club. I suppose it is the level of accomplishment, and the fact that you know that if you stick it out, you can get things done.

There is a saying in scouting that it prepares you for life, and that is true because of all the different experiences you have had on your journey. That is why Scouts are people who think about more than just themselves. You learn to think beyond just yourself and more about all the things that you can do for others, from citizenship in the nation to citizenship in your community.

At a young age, I had to fulfill my merit badge. I had to sit in a city council meeting, and this was during the Harold Washington era. I remember the aldermen yelling at each other and standing on desks, screaming at each other. I was in an observation room at the back watching the whole thing, and I asked one of the parents if this happened a lot.

They said not always, but it was an interesting awakening of how adults could behave and the different sides of politics. I have so many treasured events that happened to me during scouting, from seeing politicians operate to learning how to design a house from scratch using drafting tools.

I designed the plan for a house from scratch. One of my merit badge counselors was an engineer and draftsman, so he was skilled in how to do scale drawings. When I started on my architectural merit badge, he said, "We are going to learn it the right way", so we actually did it to scale. I did multiple levels of dimension to the drawing of that house.

It is those types of things that opened my eyes, and it is probably why I'm more likely to tinker on things now. My dad was a do-it-yourself kind of guy, too, and what I ended up learning from him was valuable to me as well.

I remember working on our basement with my dad at a young age. There were tree roots that broke the plumbing, would stop it up, and water would back up into the basement. My dad would get the rooter, and we would rod out the roots from the tree. Combining those experiences with scouting encouraged my interests and ability to fix things myself. It is always easy to call somebody and have them come fix something, but I like to give it a shot myself. Sometimes I might get into it a little too deeply and then need to call an expert, but in most cases, I have learned to fix things on my own.

I attribute scouting to part of that. I also attribute that to the way my dad worked with us when we were kids, and he allowed us to fail a lot. Scouting was the same way. It gives us a safe area to be able to fail, a place where you know that if you flip the boat in the middle of a lake, it is a lot easier than if it is the ocean.

I have a passion for boating, and now it is a matter of passing it along to my kids, so they can develop that passion if they so choose. It has been great to see them grow in this sport.

It is a very liberating feeling to have the wind in your hair, to be quiet, and to listen to the water as it ripples along the hull of the boat. Whoever would have thought that sailing that little sunfish would lead to crossing the Pacific Ocean three times, racing across Lake Michigan 21 times, and sailing in the Atlantic from St. Petersburg to Havana and from Newport, Rhode Island, to Bermuda?

The possibilities that opened from that one invitation were limitless. I am sure that no one would have imagined that

that one invitation would lead to a new world of science and travel and discovery.

Through the benefit of having had the mentors that I received in scouting, a whole new world was opened up to me. I am reminded of this when I go to speak at Schools on career development and the art of possibility.

An exercise that I love to do with kids is I walk the entire classroom out in the hallway, and I show them all the doors. I use the doors as a metaphor for the options that they need to keep in their lives.

"Your life is like this hallway, and your job is to keep as many of these doors open to you throughout your life. What keeps them open or closes them are the decisions you make during your life. It is about keeping your options open," I would tell them.

I am fortunate that some of those decisions were influenced by adults that had my greater good in mind. I understand that just that simple act is a privilege. I strongly believe that it is my responsibility to give that same privilege back to others that are less fortunate than I.

CHAPTER 5:

LIFE IS ABOUT DECISIONS WITH ASSISTANCE FROM THE LITTLE ANGELS WHO GUIDE YOU

"It is in your moments of decision that your destiny is shaped." ~ Tony Robbins

My high school years were not only formative years, which I will get into later, but they were full of experiences that built my character and shaped who I would become. Some of the most influential included my continued time with Boy Scouts, playing sports (especially baseball), and my guidance counselor, but it was a decision my friends and I made that determined the path we would later follow.

I think of us as the Five Friends. We met and became friends in part through scouting. It was natural that we would grow up together and play baseball together. We came from the same background with working-class families and parents who worked in either the steel mill or the ancillary metal foundries nearby.

We played outside together all day long throughout the summers. Some of us went to summer camp, but we all went to the park for free swim at 2 o'clock, and we loved jumping off the diving boards at the pool at Russell Square Park. For kids from the city, this was our neighborhood haven, our escape from the hot concrete during the summers in Chicago.

We did everything together, from walking on the lakefront, going to the movies, jumping on the train, going downtown, and watching the James Bond movies at the old Oriental theater downtown. There was always something to do.

At other times, we would roam the neighborhood, do boy things, and get in a little bit of trouble sometimes, but nothing major. The one rule that our parents had was to be home when the streetlights went on.

The day came when our friendship changed, and our group split. It was the summer between eighth grade and high school, and we were hanging out like we always did. Three of us who, incidentally, had stuck with baseball said we had to head home because the streetlights had come on.

THE BIG DECISION

It was the same decision we made every night, saying we have to walk home from wherever we were, so we don't get in trouble and grounded. The two other guys who, until that night, also went home, decided they were going to stick around and hang at the park.

The split had begun, and now there was distance between us. They started getting involved with gangs in our neighborhood. The break in our friendship was a challenge, and it hurt us that we couldn't get them back. I remember how we saw them at the park once and went up to them to say, "Hey, are we not friends anymore? What's the deal?" They told us, "You guys are just squares; these are our friends now. We're not going to hang out with you anymore."

So, the three of us went our way. They, like myself, were going to private schools, and our other two friends were going to go to public school. I guess that was another kind of split.

THE GANG SHOOTING

The differences transcended the schooling and the activities–it was just a start. Later we would learn that, sadly, one of our two friends shot a cop and went to jail, serving a life sentence. The other one was killed in a gang shooting, and I still remember the day it happened. We had a little league baseball game going on, and his brother played with our team. Suddenly, in the middle of the game, we heard the pop of a gunshot, and everybody hit the ground.

As the shots rang out, we all tried to stop his brother from leaving the game, telling him not to run toward the problem, but he didn't listen. I followed him, saying, "You can't go there. You don't know what's going on."

It turned out that his brother had been shot and was taking his last breaths. He died there on the sidewalk, laying halfway on the concrete and halfway in the vacant lot- in a growing puddle of blood. That fundamentally changed his life, and he went down his own route because he didn't want to be anything like what his brother ended up being.

I didn't know until the night of his wake that he had protected us from the gang, often telling them not to mess with the three of us because we were going places and would be getting out of Chicago. In a way, that bond remained from afar. Perhaps he joined so that we did not have to, he served as our shield.

For the three of us that were left, it was very clear that we made the right choice to go home. Not that we felt that we were better than everyone else, but losing those two friends broke my heart. The two remaining friends entered the working world—one is very accomplished and works for the municipal sector, and the other is a respected professional as well.

When I go to schools to speak, and try to influence young kids, I tell this story because life is all about the decisions we make. We all have the same potential. Life is ultimately a compendium of the decisions that we make and the consequences that stem from those decisions. It became very real to me that the decisions on my side of town had grave consequences. This weighed on me throughout my acculturation into mainstream America. I left my neighborhood when I moved up to the North Side to go to college. The more I interacted with some of my friends from the suburbs, the more it became apparent that my upbringing was different. Some call it trauma, I like to refer to it as lesson scars. It's what toughens us up.

When I think back to those years, I wonder what it would have been like to not lose those friends to the penal system and the grave. It's pretty impactful to have that happen at the age of thirteen-fourteen years. It weighs on you. As I encountered others later in life, I buried those memories deep. People seem to get weird when you share those types of memories with them; you are treated like you're different, and you are—but fundamentally, they treat you with either pity or awe.

VISITING AN OLD FRIEND IN JAIL

The other friend who stayed out late at the park that night also joined a gang. He ended up shooting a cop and went to jail and got a life sentence. I remember his cousins telling me that I should go visit him because, at one time, he was my best friend, and I had shut him out of my life after he went downstate.

But then, later in life, I decided to go downstate and visit him. It was an awkward discussion because our lives had gone down such different paths at that point. I was an undergrad, studying to be a doctor, and he's in jail. We had grown completely apart. Two drastically different worlds. I remember covering up my trip to the pen from my college friends so they wouldn't think that I was weird. I drove the whole way downstate–three hours each way–to see him. Plenty of time to think there and back.

As I look back, it's easy to see that even though he saw our friend die that day, it didn't change the trajectory of his life. He continued in the gang life, and a few years later, junior or senior year, we heard that he got involved in shooting a cop. He was tried as an adult and sent to state prison.

Going to see him was difficult because you could see that the penal system had hardened him. He said I talked differently, and I remember asking him to clarify what he meant by the comment that I sounded "white." He told me that I talk like I'm white, and I said, "I don't know that I've ever not talked this way."

"But now," he said, "It's more so, and I don't understand what you're saying."

It bothered me because my dad used to tell me when I went back to college, "Don't forget where you came from, and don't think that you're better than everybody."

It really bothered me that he had that perception of me

because, at one point, we were friends, and on top of that, we had this history, this part of our youth that we cherished. Rick confirmed that they had watched over us from afar. He said it with a tone of pride in his voice, "You squares were the real thing." That summer of hanging out then, it just broke, and their lives went in a completely different direction.

I remember the one question I asked him. I said, "Rick, if you had to do it all over again, would you go home? Would you have gone home when the lights went on?"

He said, "I can't change that. I can't change that. All I can do is the best with what I have now."

I think I tried to learn from what happened to him and learn a little bit more about how to make better decisions from seeing him fall. I learned his lesson for him. Maybe we all learned some lesson from them, but that was the one conversation that we did have.

He ended by saying, "Hey, man, you know I wish you well but don't ever feel sorry for me. I'm in here, and it is what it is. I'll probably never get out, you know?" I haven't gone back since because the last thing he said was, "Just forget about me."

LEARNING MORE THAN BASEBALL

As I made the transition from grammar school to high school, I was still playing baseball. I'd always grown up playing little league, and I was an ok athlete. I tried to have fun with the sport, collected baseball cards, and went to baseball games with my grandfather and my dad.

I played football first when I went to high school, and then in the spring, I tried out for the baseball team. I knew the coach because he was not only my biology teacher freshman year, but he was also an assistant coach on our football team.

The day came, and I tried out for the baseball team. When I found out I didn't make the team, I thought, I'll just try out again next year. I went to the coach after biology class one day and asked, "Hey, Mr. Lane, can you tell me what I have to do to get better, to get on the team?"

He said, "No, man, you're great." I asked again, "OK, is there anything I can improve on to get onto the team next year?"

That's when he told me, "No, we have enough of your kind." I asked him to clarify for me what he meant by "my kind?" I said, "Do you mean third basemen?" He said "No. Spics, we have enough Spics on the team." I remember the sting of the words as he said them. I looked at him, trying not to make contact with his eyes that were receded behind thick coke bottle eyeglasses.

Just as I was going to ask why he felt that, students walked into the biology classroom. I believe they were there for the next class. I tunneled out of the room and into the hall–I was short of breath and angry. I ran to the men's bathroom and into a stall to gather myself. It was another one of those times you realize you're different. I never looked at myself that way, and I was crushed. Not that I did not know I was Hispanic, but to have that weaponized against me. To be used as a criteria for selection was something I had not experienced. I took the bus home, walked into the house, and I'm pretty sure my mom could see that I was not happy because I just walked right through the house and upstairs to my bedroom.

My Uncle Frank was over that night for dinner, and he was very instrumental in my upbringing. He's the one that challenged me—he would buy me erector sets and different things to challenge my mind. He would often correct my English to make sure that there was no slang, and I didn't use contractions. He constantly challenged me to raise my standards for the world that I would live in someday.

My dad was working a double shift that night, so my mom must have asked my uncle to come upstairs. He said, "Hey, what's going on?" I told him nothing, but he didn't believe me. So, I told him the story, and he said, "That's going to happen sometimes, and you're going to feel horrible, angry. I want you to get everything out now. Cry, do what you have to do. But tomorrow, you're going to wake up, and you're going to do everything you can to be better than you are today. Don't let anybody tell you you're not going to get into someplace because of who you are or things you can't control. You show them what they missed."

After that, I started doing my own training. I obviously tried to excel in baseball to the point where next year, when I tried out, they would want me on the team. There were a couple of Mexican adult men's league teams that played at the park, so I would go and practice with them. By older, I mean in their 20s and 30s, and they would hurl 80-90 mile an hour fastball pitches. They were throwing heat, and I got used to that.

I also played with our park's Connie Mack team. My little league coach was also the coach for that team and we ended up going to the all-area finals. It was there we played a team coached by our high school's coach, and we beat them straight out that summer

Then the next school year started. It was my sophomore year—I played football and hockey, and then it was time for baseball tryouts again. I was happy after beating him in August; it was a good feeling. He approached me in the hallway after one of his classes, and he told me I should try out for the team.

I answered, "Actually, I'm not going to."

He couldn't believe it. He told me I was amazing in the all-area series and asked why not? I told him, "Because you already have enough of my kind, remember?" And I never played organized baseball again.

For me, that was my uncle's challenge, to do what you need to get there. It wasn't enough to say that I beat him. It was an incident where you can either be defeated by it, be hateful, or you can channel it and use it to overcome something—to be tenacious and persevere.

FINDING OUT WHAT I WAS MEANT TO BE

The other person that made a fundamental impact on me in high school was my guidance counselor, Mr. Capello. I was very dejected when I got the results from the career aptitude tests that would tell you what profession you should choose, and what you might want to study.

We took it our freshman year, and mine was horrible. It said I should be a car mechanic or repair guy-something where I used my hands to fix things. I took the piece of paper into my guidance counselor's office, who also happened to be my football coach.

He took it, folded it, put it in a file, and said, "That's the last time I'm going to pull that out. I don't want you to limit yourself by what a piece of paper tells you. Our job here in the next four years is to figure out exactly what you should be, what you were put here on this planet for, and how to make the best of it."

That's where we went. He helped me pursue that passion for science, that love for science that I had. I looked forward to my monthly meetings with him because he would always challenge me—not only on the field (he was relentless as my defensive coach) but he would challenge me in the classroom, in the hallways, and say quit screwing around–stick to your plan, Sandoval.

My sophomore year, there was a kid who was a bit of a troublemaker. We had co-ed gym together, and one of those scary activities in co-ed gym is dance—the waltz, the foxtrot, and dancing with a girl in front of everyone else.

One day during dance class in the gym, that kid and I ended up in a fight. I don't remember exactly how it started, but it might have been over a girl or him just not liking me.

He thought I had cut in line, which I was not about to do. If anything, I would have gone the other way, anything to save the humiliation of having to dance.

He decided to push me, and my first instinct was to step away. He decided to lunge at me a second time, and I used his momentum to knock him to the ground. Of course, the gym teacher came over and told us to go see Mr. Foster, another one of the football coaches.

Mr. Foster sat back in his chair and asked me to explain what happened. I told him that I didn't hit the kid; I only used his momentum to knock him down and get out of his way. Kind of like we learned in football, when trying to penetrate the backfield, don't fight the pulling guard or pulling tackle-use their size and momentum against them. I said I was not about to throw a punch, and Mr. Foster told me he was glad I had not done that.

He told me I was going to have a lot of times in life when people would provoke me or challenge me to do something I probably shouldn't. He said that's 100% in your control, how you react to it. You can take the provocation, or you can choose to do it a different way. "Don't let circumstances goad you into being who you are not" he would say. He went on to say that I was a student-athlete, a leader in the school, and added that leaders don't get themselves into those types of situations.

He said, "When you see those things happening, you have to remove yourself from the situation. I'm going to send you home today, and tomorrow you have to come back with your mom."

This is the second time in my life I had been sent home ever, first time for a fight. I couldn't go to football practice that day, and I got home early. I had to explain what happened to my mom, and that whole week I was made to do punishment drills in football. I had to do extra runs and drills for making a stupid decision. I ran that week until my legs hurt, until I had cramps in my sides from all the running.

When my mom came in with me the next day, Mr. Foster said, "I'm proud of your son, that he didn't throw a punch, but he does have to be a better judge of how he reacts to this type of situation." I remember looking askew at my mom, to try and catch the expression on her face. A partial 'proud smile' came onto her face which she quickly turned into a smirk when I caught her eye.

MORE CHALLENGES AHEAD

My relationship with Mr. Capello continued to blossom throughout high school. He was always really good at making sure that he challenged me to think more about everything I did, including my Eagle Scout project.

He would constantly challenge me to think, to not do the easy things, but to do those things that challenged me a little bit. He always used to say, "When you're uncomfortable, you grow." And he would always tell me to be as uncomfortable as possible because it was a sign that I was growing.

As a result, I have done that throughout my life. As I got older, I took that to mean the road less traveled, the one where nobody goes, is the path that usually leads to the highest fruit, the highest risk/reward.

As we got close to graduation, I received a football scholarship to a D3 school, but they didn't have the major that I wanted. It was then that Mr. Capello had a heart-to-heart talk with me about the realities of playing football beyond college and the possibility that I could get redshirted or worse yet, injured, and never even play in college.

He said, "You are 5 foot 8 and 140 pounds. There's not a strong chance that you would continue to play ball beyond college or even high school. Your speed makes up for what you don't have, your desire fuels you but there is a strong chance you would not play many games or maybe not even play at all in college. Your heart makes up the difference."

Mr. Capello was right, I didn't start a lot in high school football, but that didn't stop me from showing up to practice each of the four years I was on the team and practicing like I had a chance to. I would usually sub in, but I only started one game, my junior year. I knew it was my weight, no matter how much I ate and worked out, I couldn't keep weight on. A problem I wish would have followed me in life.

I was a good student, and he suggested I pursue an academic scholarship. A few weeks later, I found out I had received an academic scholarship to DePaul University. I took that and was able to study pre-med there as I had wanted to.

I remember one of the last conversations I had with Mr. Capello. He told me I had done well in high school, that I had learned a lot, and said he was amazed at how much I had grown as an individual. The day he said that to me, he had a full fat lip from a pinch of chew that he had in his mouth, "come here kid" as he gave me a huge hug. "I'm so proud of you, you should be proud of you. You have made good of your time here. You are one of our best."

"But," he added, "I'm going to challenge you to go one step further in life. Make a list of all the things you want to do before you die. It's best to do it right now while you have the whole world in front of you because that list may end up being a mile long. Then, every chance you get, look at it and knock something off that list. Try to knock something off every year or two and never let it be said at the end of your life that you lived with a 'what if.'"

Those were his last words to me. I went to his funeral a few years ago, and I told his son my story. He said we have a lot of those stories about my dad. I made that bucket list, and I've done a lot of them, including sailing across the ocean and climbing a major mountain top (Mount Rainier).

I also had jumping out of an airplane on that list, so I jumped out of an airplane not once, but 48 times. I also had 'Go to China' on the list. I didn't make it to China, but I did go to Japan and Europe to see the mountains, which were impressive, and I decided to ski them. I turned into a decent skier, and I've skied nearly most every major resort in the Western United, Canada, and Italy.

I also added softer goals like having a family, making an impact on your family's life, making an impact on a child's life, giving back, and giving back to those that gave to you–to your parents. That's still work in progress. I remember spending some key time with my dad. To try and learn his story. Growing up, I had a bit of resentment, like a spoiled brat, that he never attended my sporting events. But being a father now, I know how much was on his plate. The nice thing was that I never wanted in life growing up. He put it all on the line for us so that we could have what he didn't achieve with his eight-grade education.

As I looked back at my list when the oldest of my two daughters was going to be born, I started seeing a lot of what you see today in the news--gun crime, young men throwing their lives away in gangs and in jail, and all kinds of things. I said to myself, well, since I'm probably only going to have two daughters, I think it is time for me to try to impact the men that will be out there.

That's when I got back involved with Boy Scouts. I got into leadership, and I tried to make a foundational difference in communities. I did that for close to 11 years and retired in 2016. I needed to make an impact. It was on my bucket list and I sought to give back, not so much because of the bucket list, but because I wanted to give back to the organization that I felt fundamentally changed my life on multiple levels; morally, spiritually and that supported the values that I was raised with.

IT TAKES A VILLAGE

The ups and downs of the tumultuous economics in the

steel industry during the eighties made for some interesting challenges at times. Having four mouths to feed didn't make it easier for my parents. The transition from Cottage Grove heights in the summer of 1978 went well, but what made it better is that we moved into a block and area with instant community. As is usually the case with ethnic neighborhoods in Chicago, everything revolved around parishes.

For us, that epicenter was St. Michael the Archangel parish on 83rd and South Shore Drive. St. Michael's was a potpourri of cultures. Originally a parish built by Polish immigrants, when we arrived, the neighborhood was transitioning to a blend of Polish, Irish, Mexican and later Haitian residents. It was all centered around our Catholic faith, and it was not uncommon for our annual parish bazaar to be a feast of international delicacies—pierogies, czernina (duck blood soup), soda bread, corn beef, tamales, pozole, and, later, jerk chicken.

The church was also host to our Scout Troop 750, and the same carried over–we had a mix of kids from various backgrounds led by some amazing volunteers who gave freely of their time to Scouts, Knights of Columbus, and other traditional institutions that supported the parish.

While the intersectionality of diverse groups can sometimes be sticky, groups tended to bond based on their ethnicity. Tensions between the old guard–the Polish original residents who ran the church, the school, and pretty much everything else, there were tensions at times because of the change that was underway in the neighborhood as more Mexican-American families moved in.

My parents were accepted and bonded well into the Guadalupanos group (Supporters of Our Lady of Guadalupe) named after the matron virgin of Mexico. They convived and supported each other's families through a tight network where they supported Spanish mass on Sunday morning and all the cultural holidays for our part of the community.

One of the figurehead families in this group was the Arias Family who happened to be our next-door neighbors. Mr. Miguel Arias, was a union organizer for the AFL-CIO and head of a large family of six (two sons, four daughters). Our families became close as we had children of similar ages. One of their daughters was a few years older than I and attended my high school and later DePaul, so we always had a reference point. Their third daughter, Rocio, was a year ahead of me in high school. As is often the case when you are the first to go to college, you need someone that can buoy and guide the way. The Arias family was just that for me.

My mom had a high school education and my dad an eighth-grade education so navigating the college prep, scholarship, and application process was all new. The Arias family was also more practical in their support from math tutoring to supplement my early challenges to offering opportunities to make money doing odd jobs such as stuffing mailing envelopes, canvassing flyers, or even being stand-ins on picket lines. The little bits of help went a long way, especially during the tough times of company shutdowns when cash was tight. On a fundamental level, their support of small things like lending us a typewriter for homework (we couldn't afford one) and term papers was a huge help.

During my Senior year, I remember hearing about the LULAC scholarships (League of United Latin American Citizens) from Mr. Arias. Via the guidance from Mr. Cappello and Mr. Arias' daughter, I was able to learn about the opportunity and craft my application essay, packet, and letter. There was no doubt that without their help, I would not have been able to receive that scholarship. They were also instrumental in helping me Navigate the Pell grant applications, and other scholarship applications which later became the reason why college became achievable and a reality.

When I later sought out becoming a Resident Advisor at DePaul, it was because of having heard Maria, one of the Arias sisters, speak of her experience as an RA at DePaul. It prompted me to seek that opportunity out when I needed to move on campus to better focus on my studies. Their ongoing support and encouragement were fundamental to the community values that helped make our upbringing fruitful and helped keep us on the right track.

THE UNLIKELY MENTOR

In the Summer after graduating from high school, I sought out to get a summer job to make a little money to help with school books in college. I dabbled in a few gig jobs before I stumbled upon an ad in our local community newspaper, the Daily Calumet, for a part-time retail sales clerk at a men's store on Commercial Avenue in South Chicago.

I remember the day I walked in with the ad and asked to speak with the store manager, a tall thin man named Harold. He was seated in the shoe area of the store with Less and Kevin who were two other salesmen in the shop. Howard's was a men's outfitter that sold work clothes, suits, sport clothes, and accessories. It was named after the owner, Aaron Derman's eldest son.

After a brief conversation with the three salesmen, I was introduced to Mr. Derman in his office, a backroom of the store. Because I had basically no work experience, their questions revolved around what type of student I was, what kind of grades I got, and what other activities I took part in. This, of course, allowed me to talk about my desire to be a doctor, my pathway to becoming an Eagle Scout, what I had learned, and what I envisioned my future career to be.

The sales guys were a bit indifferent. Their most challenging question was whether I had known the previous part-time sales clerk, Nacho, who had left to pursue his studies. I found the question odd, but their rationale was that Nacho was Hispanic and because our community was so tight, they assumed we might know each other.

Mr. Derman took to my desire to be a doctor, as he had three sons—Howard, Gordie (Gordon), and Daniel—who had all gone on to be prominent physicians. He dove into a story of how friends in his community had helped his sons with their applications to medical school, and how you have to have community to achieve.

After a brief conversation, he stood up and asked when

I could start. "When do you need me," I asked. "Can you work on Friday afternoon?" said Derman. And that was the start of my career at Howard's Store for Men where I would work part-time into my freshman year at college and later turn the job over to my brother, where he would work at the store for some time until going to college.

I could write chapters about my experiences at Howards, because of the rich tapestry of community, the men's chats during slow times and my various unique experiences during my two years there. What made that time the most special is what I learned about Aaron Derman, his tenacity and resilience, and how it impacted my desire to persevere.

Aaron Derman fled Nazi occupation of Poland and the concentration camps that destroyed the Jewish community. In their early 20s, Aaron and his wife, Lisa, left Europe in 1947 with hundreds of refugees fleeing the Jewish slums of Slocum for a better life in America. He would tell me stories of their trek through Europe to flee Nazi persecution which had claimed the lives of his family. Sometimes, over a maduro wrapped number 5 Dominican Cigar (Aaron's favorites) from Gatey's shop, Aaron would share, vulnerably, the feelings he had for the atrocities that he had undergone.

I, of course, was interested in how he was able to survive given the insurmountable odds. "When it is you or the enemy, it pushes you to do things you are not proud of, inhuman things," he said tearfully, adding, "I ask for forgiveness from God every day." He showed me scars and a tattoo where he was marked by the Nazis. It left an indelible impression upon me that human beings could be so terrible to each other. Yet, out of that struggle so much desire to give back was created.

Aaron was a man who was short in stature with gray temples and a balding head. He had his signature mustache, which he would show me from a photo of him and Lisa that he carried in his wallet. It was a photo shortly after their arrival in the US. "I carry it to remember, because in remembering, you give honor to those who died so that I might live," he said.

In his lessons, his tutelage of me, Aaron was a giant among men. I admired his passion, his business intellect, and his humanity so much. It would only be natural that he would write the recommendation for my medical school applications. I remember the day that I asked him to do that for me. I was afraid that he might say no. I went into his office on a quiet afternoon, many years after I had stopped working at Howards. The store had seen its share of challenges because of ongoing economic struggles in the steel mills, and many of Howard's clientele were neighbors and employed by the steel mills.

"Sure, I will. I will pay the favor forward, but you have to promise me that you will not open the envelope," he said. A few days later, I picked up the recommendation and honored Aaron's request. Because of my workload and studies, I sent a letter to him to announce my acceptance. I sent it to his condo in Hollywood, Florida, as he had taken to spending more time there. Weeks later I would receive a very nicely written letter back from him telling me how proud he was of the man I had become and how it was an honor to have crossed paths. He closed his letter with the words "Lekh Lekha," which translates to go forth, so I did.

Over a decade later, I would cross paths with Daniel Derman, Aaron's son during travels at Northwestern Memorial Hospital with one of my field sales reps. I made it a point to tell him how impactful his Dad was and how much I valued him. Mr. D was living in Florida mostly at that time and had long since sold the store and building. Aaron and Lisa's story of perseverance is enshrined at the National Holocaust Museum so that others may remember and be inspired, much like he inspired this kid from the South Side. I later learned that Aaron moved on to a higher place in 2005. He has visited me in my dreams at times. In those dreams I've thanked him and asked him what the letter said. "I think you know," he responded.

When I speak for youth organizations, and tell them about mentorship and people in my life, I say, "You know what? Sometimes we have to look for mentors that may not look like us. I've been fortunate to have many of them—the Mr. Capello's, the Mr. Jamrozy's, and Mr. Czjakowski's of the world, my Scoutmasters, my uncle, my grandfather, and my dad. The Aaron Derman's, and the Arias Family–those were the people in my life who cut the path for me, who kept me on the straight and narrow. Their grace and compassion have allowed me to go forth. I have been blessed beyond them into adulthood with many sponsors who have advocated for me and spoke my praises when I'm not in the room."

Life is truly about the decisions we make and the little angels who guide us along the way.

Chapter 6

46 NO'S AND THEN A YES

"Fall Seven Times and stand up eight"

~ Japanese Proverb

Everything about medicine fascinated me, especially the way that the human body was a complex system of cells, nerves, and organs all working in an orchestrated symphony. After graduating from DePaul University's pre-med program with a degree in biochemistry, my plan was to be a physician. I had dreamed of this since the days when I would look into a microscope to try and identify the various cell samples taken from my recently deceased goldfish.

I was fortunate to have had the opportunity to study biochemistry under some amazing mentors in both the biology and chemistry departments of the university. I was blessed with some great referrals and recommendations and had done a lot of co-op work during my undergrad. This made it possible for me to be accepted into medical school at Loyola Medical Center.

I didn't receive notice of my formal acceptance until June as I was waitlisted originally, and it was going to be a stretch to start by late August. I already had an internship at Argonne National Laboratory in Darien, Illinois and the professor I was working with, Dr. Claudia Libertine, was on faculty at Loyola in the Dept. of Infectious Disease.

I was working on my thesis most of that summer, commuting to Loyola and then back to Argonne. During that time, we were working on the early tumor markers for cancer cells. The significance of this fascinated me. It was all straight research, studying markers in the brain cells of mice that were bred for that specific purpose. My job as a researcher was to harvest the brain cells. The process involved extracting the cell in the marker itself biochemically, tagging it with a radio-isotope, and measuring the levels of isotope to identify the number of cancerous cells. We would then freeze the solution of cells and, later on, look at them with an electron microscope.

We would then aggregate the data, analyze the results against the thesis of the study, and publish the findings via a research paper. It was very intense work, with a lot of insight. Much of the research was funded by private industry which worked well inside of the public-private model. The great part was that on the clinical side of things, I got a chance to see the real-world application of much of this.

THE EVOLVING WORLD OF HEALTHCARE

The world of healthcare was going through some major changes during the late eighties and early nineties. During conversations with different colleagues, people I knew that had gone to medical school a year or two ahead of me, I started to gain insight on their individual disenchantment with the field of medicine. Many of these friends had completed medical school and were going into their residency programs.

The changing landscape of medicine represented the growth of HMOs (health maintenance organizations) which were impacting the reason why many of us were going into medicine to begin with–to help and cure people. The limitations physicians were seeing from restrictions on range of care, capitation rates, and limits imposed to control escalating costs were a bit more than some of my med school pals wanted. Many of them were considering fields such as surgery and sub-specialization that took them away from the front lines which is what fueled our passion for the profession.

Physicians going into healthcare were thinking, "I'm a cog in the wheel," and as I talked to more and more of my colleagues, they were saying, "This is very disenchanting. As we're coming out of medical school, there are fewer private practices because they're all being bought up by these large conglomerates. You then become an employee, and it's just about seeing patients for two seconds. You can't see them for any longer than that because the business side of it is based on you have to spend X amount of time with a patient, and anything beyond that impacts your productivity."

Doctors at that time were starting to have this realization that it's not so much about the quality of care and being able to spend time talking with patients and helping them get better. It's like making donuts and rushing to take a bathroom break, then rushing back to make the donuts because, at the end of the day, your productivity is based on the number of donuts that you make, not the quality of the donuts.

That got me thinking. Do I really want to be a doctor and go through another eight years of school only to be a cog in the wheel? I was having an epiphany because, at this time, the company my dad worked for, US Steel, was going through its own transition because of a collision between the interests of labor unions and the impact of foreign steel on jobs on the South Side of Chicago.

It was the first time my dream was challenged. It made me ask, did I want to lead a life where a corporation governed my life? I thought I had it all figured out, but the plan was being challenged. What did I really want to be when I grew up? All these years, I thought I wanted to be a doctor because it would allow me to follow my passion, which is helping people. But suddenly, that appeared to be a fallacy.

I was in my early 20s, a time when you're very idealistic. You see the world and look for a way to help, to make an impact. And then you have a realization, the veil gets pulled back, and you see what the world is really about. For me, that was an eye-opener.

Did I want to be a doctor any longer? I was falling out of love with medicine, but the business side still intrigued me. It was the entrepreneurial side of me that has always been there, even as a kid selling cookies and candies so that I could go to camp. I had dedicated so much time to this field of medicine and my studies–for what?

After much thinking, some tears and the stark realization, I had made my decision, and now I had to stiffen up my spine and go to tell my dad that I was not going to be a doctor. This came at a hard time for my dad. He was the sole breadwinner in the house and now, suddenly, he'd been laid off, or the unions locked themselves out of the company, and here I *was*, bringing unexpected negative news.

So, we sat down and had a long conversation at the kitchen table about what I thought being a doctor would be, and what the reality was. It was hard for my parents to hear that, but after a long uncomfortable pause my dad said, "OK, that's fine, but you're not going to sit on the couch for the whole summer," and I said I wouldn't. I still had to finish my internship, my thesis, and writing my term papers. There was much work to finish.

I started talking about all the different things I could do—get my Ph.D., maybe go into industry and do research for a different company, maybe this or that. I was hitting them with a lot. So, I took some time to think, to journal my thoughts, and write out my options.

It was up to me to back out of medical school. So, I went to them and said I wanted to pull out of medical school. They asked why, and I explained that my eyes had been opened to what it was really about. Then, I had all these doctors all leaning in. I told them that I'd watched and known it was more about moving through and less about the care of people.

As a parent, I've been placed in some similar scenarios and I now know what it must have felt like for my parents to get this feedback, to have their dreams for me changed. The wonderful thing about all of this is that they provided me with ample grace and the ability to make my own decisions. It took me back to the days of helping dad do projects where he'd let me fail and then he'd sit me down, and say what did you learn?

Except, here the learning wasn't in play, the lesson wasn't complete, and I had no crystal ball to see how this would turn out. I just had my gut, the research I had done on the issue, the data that I collected, and my faith. So, after some huge prayers, I threw myself forward into my decision without knowing my outcome. Just living my life. Understanding that I might fail, but it was my decision.

A NEW OPPORTUNITY

So that summer continued on and one day, upon returning from work, there was a telegram. A big yellow Western Union telegram, at my parents' house. I opened it up, and it read, *"Dear Mr. Sandoval, we'd love the opportunity to meet with you. You had an interview on campus when we were there to visit, and we would like to talk to you about a new program that we're starting. It's a management professional development program for high potential undergrads who majored in science and have strong leadership potential and leadership capabilities."*

The company that sent me the invitation was Abbott Laboratories, located in North Chicago, in Lake County, Illinois. I drove all the way up there from the South Side of Chicago, and it took forever. I thought, I'm not going to do this every day. At that time, I didn't know if I wanted to go into the program, if it was for me. I remember pulling up to the luxe corporate campus—everything was first rate–and there was a name badge at the front gate when I checked in. I was directed to the building where I would be meeting with the recruiter.

I met my interviewer at the main building, a gentleman by the name of Keith Allen. I remember how patient he was with me, the neophyte. I then spent the entire day going through a round of interviews. At the end of the day, I was dispatched to go home and, a couple of days later, I got a call. They said congratulations, we'd love to offer you the position to enter the program. My first assignment was to be at the headquarters in the diagnostics division. From there, I would be doing six-month rotations through different positions, in different parts of the company.

This sounded interesting, and luck seemed to be on my side. I accepted the job, and things were going great, even though I was still driving every day from the South Side. It was quite an experience and everything I thought it would be. It was very exciting, too, at the age of 21, to get an assignment in Germany to work at one of the facilities on a product transfer. I was also fortunate to work on projects in Japan, Puerto Rico, and Dallas.

Throughout much of this, I received enviable mentoring and talent guidance. Because of the position, I was able to get coaching from the divisional vice president and presidents on my presentation skills. Some of the mentors that I had back then went on to fill very big roles in the company. One of my mentors went on to be the CEO of the corporation in later years.

Some of the valuable management experience that I received early on came through these mentoring sessions. As I look back, it was foundational in my development as a business person and leader at a very impressionable stage.

HONOR YOUR HERITAGE

As one of the few Hispanics in the program, it required that I was very acculturated. There was very little authenticity in my roles. Most of my co-workers were not of my background and understood less of my cultural upbringing. At the operations level, some of our employees filled the line positions in our manufacturing positions. This was especially true in Lake County where most of those Hispanics were recruited right out of high school in nearby Waukegan. Working in a company like Abbott, with its robust profit-sharing program, could be transformational for those employees. I know many a person that worked line positions at Abbott for much of their career and retired millionaires from smart use of their profit-sharing plan, 401k, and benefits.

In spite of this, it never felt good not to have others like me to model and look up to. I would have to stomach microaggressions that were often laughed off as part of the job. One of those incidents came during one of my assignments where I was invited to attend a colleague's birthday party. It was held at his house in Racine, WI on a weekend.

Many of our employees lived as far away as Southeast Wisconsin due to the lower cost of living. Southeast Wisconsin had an interesting pattern of immigration–many of the immigrants that settled in that area were of German descent, drawn there by the various industrial jobs at Johnson Wax, AMC auto, and other major employers. Some were transplants from Illinois drawn the newer housing stock and schools.

I remember attending the birthday event. In spite of the rather long drive up, I had been looking forward to it, because I really liked this group I worked with. It was a jovial and fun group that spent a lot of time building camaraderie in and out of the office. Mike Seltzer was the more tenured guy in that department and the most senior. A short stocky guy, he was mid-thirties and balding. He was looked to as the "leader" in the group and supervised a few of the workgroups which added to his role. He also had considerable tenure at the company. Many of the team members in this department were in that age group – late twenties to early thirties. I was the younger guy in my early twenties.

When I started working in the group, it became common practice to ask about what your heritage was. We had a German, an Armenian, an Italian, a person with a Jewish background, and with an Irish background in the group. When I shared my background, I remember telling them that I was of Mexican descent, to which one of the team members replied, "Mexican? Like from down south, Mexico? That's far away, almost as far as Sweden. You don't look Mexican, you look Swedish–we'll call you the Swede." From that day on, my nickname became "The Swede." Perhaps it was innocent, but it may have not been. I suspected it was some sort of code because I certainly did not have Swedish features.

The day of the birthday party, as I arrived at Mike's house, much of the team was there, as were others from various production groups at the company. Mike was fairly well known. They were having a great time. There was a lot of great food, and given the nice weather that day, the party was in the backyard. I chatted with different people, trying to fit in. A group of us were on the deck with the guest of honor, Mike Seltzer.

Mike's yard had a very nice garden with some of the vegetables he was known to grow. Among this garden I was amazed at the enormous tomatoes that he was growing. They had to be as large as small cantaloupes. In the midst of the conversation and to compliment him on these tomatoes, I remember saying to Mike that I admired the size of the tomatoes he had in the garden. Mike tried to make a joke saying, "Yeah, I bet you like those tomatoes. You Swedes are pretty good at picking them aren't you? Why don't you pick me one of those?"

A lot of the team was a few beers into the afternoon, so a combination of that and Mike's humor at my expense brought on a roar from the group. I remember the feeling of humiliation at the belittling comment in front of the whole group. I didn't know where to hide, nor did I know what provoked this, but in response to Mike's comment, I walked over to the closest tomato vine, picked one up walked over to where Mike was sitting and proceeded to smash the tomato on Mike's bald, partially sunburnt head and said, "Picked just for you." The group went silent, then laughed. I said goodbye, jumped in my car, and drove home.

That next Monday, I made my usual commute to Abbott Park. I remember walking in and settling into my cube. Most of the team was in and working in the development lab. A bit later that morning, our department manager came in to ask if she could speak with me in private. We walked across the hall to her office. As she shut the door behind me, it became evident that this "coaching session" was, perhaps, a bit more. She proceeded to ask me what had happened at the birthday party that weekend. I explained the course of the event from my point of view. It became evident that she had heard of it, either from Mike or one of our co-workers.

I had a ton of respect for Cynthia Salinas. She had worked

in a hospital diagnostics lab for some time prior to coming to work for Abbott, and was originally from Texas. She was very acculturated in spite of her Tex-Mex background. Soft-spoken, but firm, she could hold her own in a room full of mostly men. She ran the process development team—which is the group where this assignment was, a group that served as the scale-up test lab for manufacturing processes as they moved from R&D to production.

"Lou, I'm going to give you some advice," she said. "Being Hispanic is going to come up from time to time. There just aren't many of us in these types of jobs. While this might be the first time that this has come up at work, you have to learn to handle these types of things differently. This happened outside of work hours, but it impacts your work environment because everyone has to get along here. Inside the work team, we can't have any of that. From what it seems, Mike should not have made those comments to you. I will speak to him about that and ask him to apologize to you. You have to learn to take the high road and not let those things get to you. Smile it off, walk it off, but don't let them know they got to you. You have more to lose, remember that."

As I walked out of the room, I knew that I was lucky it had happened outside of work. She was spot on in her feedback. While I had effectively made my point to Mike that I disapproved of his agricultural humor, he hit a raw spot. Perhaps it was the knowledge that my ancestors had once picked the fields of the plain states, or perhaps it was the realization of what being a "Swede" meant but, never-the-less, it stung, and doubly so because of the humiliation of having been the brunt of the joke in front of everyone.

Mike came up to me and apologized later that day. I apologized to him for ruining a perfectly good tomato. We smiled it off and continued in a productive work relationship for the remainder of my time in that group. I continued to be the Swede, and I seemed to be the only one with a nickname on the team.

SHIFTING GEARS

While the program I was enrolled in was to prepare me for roles in operational leadership, I received a bit of invaluable advice from one of the mentors that helped shape the trajectory of my career. One day, during a coaching session with one of our division leaders, I received the advice that, if I really wanted to go anywhere in my career, I had to look at the revenue side of the business, to fully understand the various avenues in which the company makes its money. The advice was a bit more pointed, "Favor revenue producing positions and less of the staff positions in cost centers."

By this, he meant to go into a sales and marketing career path. Abbott had a good internal placement system, and you could look at all of the jobs that were available within the company, all over the world, and you could post for them, with your supervisor's approval. By applying online, they would get you in front of people for interviews. So, every day on my lunch break, for about six weeks, I would diligently apply for every sales job I qualified for.

By this time, Abbott had grown by leaps and bounds in every one of their divisions. I would look at all of these opportunities, all the sales positions that they had, and I would keep a very meticulous list of all the jobs I applied to, including the person I sent my information to, the date of the application, whether I received an interview, and what the outcomes were of the phone screen and in-person interviews.

As I interviewed with all these different people, they all said close to the same thing--it's great that you've got all this science background and business management or leadership background, but we really need somebody with hard sales experience. The profile they tended to favor was capital equipment sales and other formal sales positions which they tended to recruit from outside of the company.

They told me that the people they were recruiting were coming from companies like Xerox and that they had sales discipline, training, and a formal sales background. I told them, I had both. I understand the science of what we're doing because I had led the development of our products, and I also have the sales side of it. I understand how to prospect, and I've been selling since I was a kid. They said, yeah, that's great but not great enough.

The list that I compiled tracking my activity became a list of rejections. At times, it seemed like a no-win situation, but I continued to identify opportunities and make the calls and connect with the hiring managers.

PERSEVERANCE PAYS OFF

As I kept on applying for jobs, the list was getting longer and longer. It was great that we had this placement system, but often it was up to me to research the positions and identify other ways of getting to the decision makers. I would leverage relationships with various product managers I worked with and had them introduce me to the regional managers.

Because it was sales, I had to keep a running organizational chart for each division and stay on top of the personnel changes as people were promoted or left. Little did I know it, but I was going through my own sort of training in lead cultivation during this time. It was what a sales territory manager would need to do when they got a territory. Identify the organizational matrix, figure out who the decision makers were, and find a way to influence them.

Finally, through this ongoing networking process, meeting different people and calling them, I had developed a collegial relationship with Keith Mallett, the original recruiter at the company who was in HR. He advised me that the pharmaceutical division of the company was going through a major expansion with the launch of some new products.

Keith connected me with the national director of sales. This was one of the advantages of being at the global headquarters, you had access to many of the executives. I networked my way into a conversation with this national director of sales, Mark Roth. He said, "I don't know how well it's going to go, but send me your resume. I'll put it in front of my regional managers. They're going to have a large meeting, and I'll put it in front of as many of them as possible."

He kept his word, and before long, I got a call from one of the regional managers on the west coast, Vic Saunders. He told me my resume was currently in front of three of his district managers, all of whom wanted to talk to me in greater depth.

We agreed they would fly me down to their national sales conference in Ft. Lauderdale, Florida, where I would meet with each of them. The openings they had were in Modesto, California, Sacramento, California, Reno, Nevada, and Seattle, Washington.

As I looked at a map, I realized that Modesto was in the middle of the desert, Sacramento was in northern California, and I'd been to Reno. Those were not places where I wanted to live, but Seattle, that area was cool, and I love the water. I was in a group that I sailed with on Thursday nights, and I was sure I could find people to sail with in Seattle. As a bonus, skiing would also be an option, another one of my favorite activities.

After an introductory phone conversation, Vic asked me to rank the different locations, and I met with all the managers, not necessarily in order of preference. From the managers in Reno, Modesto, and Sacramento, I got maybe. But the manager from Seattle, Felix Liu, had only been in his role a couple of months after graduating from the Ross School of Business graduate program at the University of Michigan, and he was hard to read.

First, he asked why I wanted to be in sales and why it would be good for the company, and then he asked the perfect question—how would you track your progress?

I said, "Pretty simply. Let me show you something. This is the list that I've been using to track the number of jobs that I've applied for, the people that have been interested, the number of phone screens I've had, what my follow-up has been, where I'm going with it, and whether I've gotten an in-person interview or not. Here's the progress of this whole journey.

He wanted to know how many people were on the list. He was impressed when I told him 45 and that he was the number 46. He said I would need that level of persistence if I got the job because the doctors I would call on were in medical districts where I would have to get by the gatekeeper in order to go back, and I would only get a few minutes to talk with them.

He added, "If you can apply a little bit of what you did in your list there and your tenacity and tracking your progress to this, I'll help you learn the rest of it." I was happy when that interview ended, because for once it felt like my luck was changing.

What is the saying? When it rains it pours? Well. It was a close call. While I had gone through a drought of 45 no's, I not only received an affirmative on the 46th attempt, but it seemed like I also got the 47th and 48th! I now had offers from the Modesto and Sacramento managers on top of the interest from the Seattle manager. I now had choices. Despite the other managers asking to hire me first, I held out for Seattle and eventually got it. Within 60 days, I had moved to a place in Seattle, sight unseen, where I had no friends or family. There was some irony in that since I had just bought a condo in Gurnee, Illinois, and had lived there less than six months when this happened.

I tend to make friends easily and in Seattle, I made a network of friends through a sport and social club that I belonged to where we played hockey, baseball, softball, and went to all kinds of social events. I also had a few work colleagues in the local Seattle area that I became good friends with.

Most of the time, though, it was nothing but work. I dug my nose down into it and got results. My hard work paid off, and I took the territory from the bottom third of the region into the top five in the region in one year by applying a lot of the same perseverance and tenacity that I had done in pursuing the job.

To this day, Felix will tell you one of the things that impressed him most was how driven and focused I was. He would often rib me and tell me that I was a work in progress on the sales side, but my tenacious approach made the difference.

HARD WORK CREATES LUCK

I once read somewhere that success occurs at the intersection of hard work and opportunity. I lived in Seattle for three years, and during that period I lived a lot. I made some great friends, I had some great success in my main career, and my side hustle grew (more on that soon). In the work and career success that I achieved, being ranked as one of the top territories in the region, was a validation for

Vic Saunders, my region manager based out of Orange County, and the chance he had taken on me.

Ultimately it was Vic and Felix who had to "bless" hiring me. They took a chance on me—a guy who came completely out of left field, didn't have a sales background, and who had potential but hadn't been trained in it. I'm sure there were probably some sweaty moments, wondering if this guy was going to work out or not.

My success on the sales side of the balance sheet eventually led to me getting promoted, then promoted again. My ambition, tenacity, and perseverance with a bit of luck created opportunities to continue to work up the ladder.

It would lead to my experiences in Seattle, Miami, and then Chicago again. The success I had in Miami, I would later replicate in management roles in both Miami and back in the home office.

Through a series of mentors that I developed along the way, I would continue to learn. I am very fortunate to have had those region managers, district managers, and regional trainers as they helped me with the first third of my trajectory.

In Miami, I would master the art once again of being an outsider—this time developing close ties with the Cuban community. I am blessed to have had the experience of living in Miami. It made me see the richness of the Latin culture with more of a Pan-American theme. The Cuban culture is very close knit, one that can be tough to crack, but when you do, you make friends for a lifetime. Some of the friends I made in Miami, I still keep in touch with. This includes the mentors I made along the way-they hold a special place in my heart. As I look back on the lessons that I learned along the way, they shaped me into who I am, and my experiences gave me a perspective that I would not trade for anything.

One of the managers that I had the pleasure of working with during my time in Florida was Jeannie Matthews. I learned tons from her. Her management style was a very nurturing one, and her philosophy is one that I later adopted in my management style. She believed very strongly that her role as leader of the team was to bring resources that would help us become successful. Those resources might be financial (e.g., budget) or in the form of tools that we could use to expand our message with our clients.

She was also very empowering. She gave success to the team, as we were the ones doing the hard work and praised early and often. The culture of the team for her was one where we worked hard, but we also celebrated our wins. Our wins were bountiful, in part because of her leadership style and because of the culture she created. You wanted to work hard for her, and you took pride in making sure that the team won to make her proud.

I carried many of these early lessons of team, culture, and empowerment forward into my roles as a leader. Aside from the formal training, the practical training I received by being exposed to some early leaders was fundamental to my development as a leader of leaders in this early phase of my career.

CHAPTER 7:

MAN PLANS, AND GOD LAUGHS

*"Sometimes good things fall apart, so better things can fall together." ~ **Marilyn Monroe***

Break-ups are hard, it's true. Certainly, it was for me. It's when you've made it through and have some distance that you can look back over that time in your life with some clarity. When I did that, I realized it was probably one of the more pivotal points in my life and what I believe drove me to become successful in my career.

After all, they say the best way to mend a broken heart is to dive into your work and try to put some separation into it. And I did, but let's back up and start at the beginning.

When I went away to DePaul for my undergrad degree,

I decided to get a job as a resident advisor. In the process of doing this, there were a lot of team-building activities so we could get to know each other. I was appointed to the third floor as the guy's resident advisor, and Janie Folk was named the girl's resident advisor for our sister floor.

A lot of times, you would do co-shifts when you had to be on duty, and you would do those shifts with a partner. So, I developed a close platonic friendship with Janie, even though she was dating a guy who was away in the military. When he returned to college, he attended Eastern Illinois University downstate, so they still had a long-distance relationship.

There were some things that weren't working out in their relationship, and because we had become close friends, she would confide in me. Because of this, I viewed her boyfriend, Lawrence, through her eyes, with her perspective, because, of course, I was only hearing one side of the story.

It wasn't long before we developed a strong friendship, and we became inseparable. Her relationship with Lawrence deteriorated over time, and he eventually broke up with her. As the friend and confidante, she confided a lot of the heartbreak to me.

It wasn't surprising that because of this, we became even closer, and a relationship developed. It feels odd when you start dating someone who's been your friend. It's just a little awkward at first, but it didn't stop us, and it didn't seem very long before love blossomed. This happened during our sophomore year of undergrad and continued through senior year. She finished a semester early but we walked in the same graduation ceremony that spring.

While I stayed in the dorm, Janie moved back home and started her graduate work. During this time, I had developed a very strong friendship not only with her but also with her family. Her two sisters felt like my sisters, and I became very close with her mom and dad as well. We would spend weekends at their lake house in Indiana.

THE COMFORT OF DISCOMFORT

It felt very comfortable for both of us, and the physical distance became a barrier. It was at this time that I began my own transition, thinking I would be going to medical school, and I began working at Abbott and digging into my career. In hindsight, this was very difficult for her when she was trying to find out who she was, and she was changing as well.

Meanwhile, we clung to the comfortable path–each other. Oddly, it was the friendship where our relationship started that was really at the core. As often happens during periods of transition, we held on to a little bit of the past–our college days and each other. In my mind, I was thinking that this seemed like somebody I wanted to spend the rest of my life with.

So, I bought a ring and proposed to her. But it was short-lived, because six months after we became engaged, she had a change of heart. I think because there had been a friendship first, she thought we could just go back to being friends, but once you've crossed that threshold, it becomes very difficult to do that.

So, there's the pain of loss, calling off the wedding, and then there was the house we had bought together. Her mom had given us money to buy a house, and it hadn't taken long to find one and start the planning process to move in. Her mom was in the real estate business, so I went to her and said, I need your help to get out of the house and mortgage. I remember the day that I went to talk to her about this. With much remorse, her mom agreed to help, and she got the paperwork ready.

Her mom was genuinely heartbroken, and I remember that when she sent me the release, she included a long letter that I kept. She told me that she would have liked it to end differently, that she knew I would do well in my life, and I would persevere. She said, "You're a very talented and bright individual. I wish that our paths would have stayed together, but we can't live our children's lives for them. It is ultimately their decision and we have to live with them." It was a heartfelt letter, and her mother was a class act.

MENDING THROUGH WORK

We went our separate ways, and my career was going gangbusters. I was traveling to Japan and Germany, and I was burying my head into my work. I think a lot of that was just to protect myself and my heart, which had been shattered. I needed to get over that so that I could forget.

I lost a lot of weight and was probably in the best shape

I've ever been in. I ran marathons and did a lot of things to help keep me focused, to keep me from feeling the pain. I think my career and my success benefited from it because I was putting one hundred percent into it with zero distractions and I definitely got one hundred percent results out of it.

Along the way, I learned that Janie had gotten back together with Lawrence, her ex-boyfriend. I also heard that her mom's breast cancer had come back–she eventually succumbed to the cancer, and it took her life. I saw Clarice as a surrogate mom, and it was painful to hear when she passed away. I visited with the family during this difficult time, and despite the awkwardness, I attended the services at a distance.

THE RECONNECTION

I don't quite remember how our paths crossed again, Janie and me. It might've been while running in Lincoln Park. We started talking, and she mentioned that she had broken up with Lawrence yet again. We started to enjoy each other's company again and, eventually, the relationship rekindled. I couldn't help but think, fool me once, shame on you. Fool me twice, shame on me.

At this point, my career was in full bloom, and I was getting ready to move to Seattle. As I'm dealing with the challenges of moving while in a relationship again, I was asking myself, what does this look like moving forward? Long-distance relationships never seem to work, but I thought, OK, we'll try it and like before we clung to the comfortable.

I had to do what was right for me, so I moved to Seattle and did my thing, but I think she was a little upset. She came out to visit one time, but we could tell the relationship wasn't the same. She had been trying to tell me the entire time that it was over, but I didn't want to admit it—probably for selfish reasons and for the lack of wanting to branch out.

After that weekend we spent together in Seattle, I came home from work one day, and there was a voicemail on my machine. The guy said, "Hi, Lou, this is Mark Campia. You don't know me, but I just wanted to let you know that I'm dating Janie. If you've got any problems with it, call me."

As you would imagine, I was surprised at first and then thought, whatever. I called her up directly to ask why, and she said she had been trying to tell me it wasn't working. I couldn't help thinking that she could have tried harder and been direct instead of wasting her time and money coming out for the weekend. I'd been down this road before, and perhaps it was the callouses that developed from the last episode, but I said fine, I wish you luck and didn't give it any more thought. My way of compensating for the loss was to bury my head in work yet again and forget the pain.

After that, my career took off, and I continued to live my life in Seattle. In a crazy twist of fate, about six months later, I was rollerblading around Green Lake when Janie's ex, Lawrence, came toward me. I was so surprised I stopped to ask what he was doing in Seattle and was even more surprised to discover he was living there.

As it turned out, we got together for a beer one day, and

I didn't find him to be a jerk, the way Janie had described him. In fact, I thought he was a cool guy, and we got to be very good friends, enough so that our friend circles in Seattle came together. To this day, we are still friends, and when he comes to Chicago or I go to Seattle, we get together. Interestingly, our birthdays are days apart so we always call each other in February. Come birthday time to catch-up, we have children around the same age, and we still have many friends in common.

There's a certain oddity that out of that heartbreak, so many things were born—my career, friendships, and I was able to accomplish so many things. All because I said to myself, nothing's going to defeat me; I'm going to bury this heartbreak, and I'm going to win, I'm going use it to drive me.

OVERBOARD

When you get out of a relationship—for the second time—it gives you a chance to look over what happened, take responsibility for your decisions, and then move on without regrets. This was another period in my life when having a bucket list gave me purpose when I needed it. One of the things I had written on my list back in high school was the goal of crossing a major ocean.

I was still feeling some shame for a second failed relationship with Janie, but it was time to move on, and thankfully I had the Compass Boat Management side hustle business to keep me busy.

At that time, I was already sailing J24s on Lake Union, but now I had access to other boats, and one of my customers asked if I had ever thought of doing any transpacific races. I hadn't, but I did have the ocean crossing on my bucket list. He suggested that a race across the Pacific would be a good opportunity to cross that off.

We agreed to do it, and I started researching what is involved in that type of race and talking to people at the yacht club. We needed to find qualified crew, get them trained, and make all the logistical arrangements for it. I also made arrangements for a series of delivery captains to sail the boat down the coast to Los Angeles, California.

I took vacation time off of work, went down to LA, and made sure that everything was ready for the race, from maintenance to stocking supplies. We also needed time to practice and get our safety at sea work formally done. The logistics of all of this was daunting. The race itself would take at least eight days on the water, and for me, that meant bundling all my vacation time and then some into this one event.

The beginning of the race is an exhilarating experience because the race leaves from Los Angeles Harbor, and you zigzag most of the time with the wind head-on as you make your way to Catalina Island. That in itself is a beautiful experience because as you make your way to Catalina and go around the island, then there are a series of islands as you make your way down into the Tradewinds.

That's really where you start to go fast. I remember the

excitement of doing that in my first Transpac race. I was exhausted because I'd been hustling for 72 hours before taking off. I'd done almost everything--the provisioning, the planning, the management—because that's what I did for the guy, right? So, for me, starting the race was the biggest sigh of relief. The hard work was done, and everyone, including the guy who owned the boat, was racing. We had a crew of strong accomplished sailors, and the owner was a great sailor and very nice guy.

He wanted to do it just because it was one of those things on his list, so we met in the middle, and that was a great way to do it. It was a 48-foot boat, which is kind of small for that event. Usually, you want a bigger boat because the waves can get fairly large. A 48 falls right in the middle for the size of the waves in a really bad situation. She was a seaworthy craft with ample space, nice amenities, and some passages of her own on her log.

We set out, and I remember the enthusiasm, the excitement, and the adrenaline rush of starting the race. That very first night, as we're heading towards Catalina Island, we were on a starboard tack, which means the wind was coming from the starboard side, the sun had just set, and it was my watch onboard.

I was with the team on deck that night, and I went forward. We had done a sail change earlier in the evening, and the sail was bagged up and on the foredeck, we wanted to retrieve it and change it out. Suddenly, we got a wave, and the deck got wet. I went forward a little bit, and I had boots on—all the gear—and I was tethered to the boat.

Suddenly, another wave came up. We hit a big wave, came down the back side of the wave, and I came up off the deck, hit the deck, and slid underneath the portside life line. Because of my tether, I was attached to the boat. The boat was on heel, and I was beneath the surface of the water getting dragged by the boat stuck against the portside hull on the leeward side.

As this was going down, I had one of those out-of-body experiences where I could see the moon. I could see the clouds. Imagine this happening under a veil of water while trying to come up for air, only I couldn't because the boat speed and hydrotension had me pinned to the hull of the boat.

As all of this was happening at what seemed like lightning speed and I was thinking, so this is how it's going to end? Then I remembered that I had tied my crew knife on my personal flotation device (PFD). I finally got it out, flipped it open, and I was exhausted. If this didn't work, I was done. Because I was trying to hold my breath, grab as much air as I could, when I could, in little bits without swallowing seawater.

I thought I could hear noise on the deck--a lot of talking, but I couldn't understand what they were saying. It turns out that they were trying to figure out where I was. After the fact, they said, we saw you disappear and thought you went overboard. And I said, well, I did, but I was still attached to the boat. They had not seen my tether drawn to the leeward side.

My last-ditch effort was to cut the tether so I could use my feet to push away. I knew that detaching from the boat might let me breathe, but it also might mean that I would be lost at sea. So, I had my choice–be drowned by the boat or take my chances in the open ocean. I gave it one last shot, cut myself free, pushed myself away from the boat, and the PFD inflated. That's when the crew saw me and immediately turned around, got a light on me, and brought me back on the boat in one figure eight rescue that made me proud that we had practiced all of that in the days prior.

Once back on board, I was absolutely exhausted. They got back on course, adjusted the trim, and just kept going. I went down below to dry off. I'm salty, just nasty, and I'm trying to gather myself. I'm thinking, wow, this is as close as I've ever come to dying, and I don't ever want that feeling again.

I stripped off my clothes, wrapped up in a blanket, and rinsed my clothes in fresh water when one of the guys came down to check on me, asking how I was doing. I said fine. A little shook up, but fine. I was just happy to be back on board the boat, and I had the realization that it didn't matter how bad my life had been up to that point or the things that I was dealing with. There was nothing better than being alive after an experience like that to put it in perspective for you.

The rest of the race was rather enjoyable given the full moon that we sailed under and warm tropical air with the spinnaker on a run. There is nothing like it, and to this day, some of my favorite sailing is under a full moon in a sea breeze.

We ended up finishing the race, and we did ok, not a personal best for anyone. Sailing into Honolulu Harbor and going into the Molokai making trees under a spinnaker was an experience like none other. I remember during my off-hours, journaling and writing some of the things about my experience, being able to look over and see Pacific Whiteside dolphins swimming alongside the boat or a huge full moon over the Pacific at night.

For me, I think it was my wake-up call to say, hey, stop wallowing in your misery. Be happy that you're alive because the alternative is obviously more consequential.

I ended up doing that race twice. I also did the Vic-Maui, from Victoria, British Columbia, Canada, down to Maui, Hawaii, and it was beautiful, just painfully long. That's a 3,800-mile race, and it was just amazing. We also did a race from Newport, California, to Ensenada, Mexico. All of those races were wonderful experiences, but thankfully uneventful compared to my first Transpac.

MANIFESTING THE BUCKET LIST

During those three years of living in Seattle, I went through this period of checking things off my bucket list at a rapid pace. I also wanted to jump out of a plane and decided to start with bungee jumping off Nanaimo Bridge in British Columbia, Canada, when we were up there for the Vic-Maui race. I think it was 125 or 175 feet above the river. They strapped you in, you jumped off the bridge, and when the bungee extended all the way, it bounced back up, and then they'd drag you off. It was an exhilarating feeling.

I don't know if it was self-destruction (I joke) or what I was looking for, but at that time, it seemed as if there was something crazy that I could do, then I was going to do it. So, of course, the next thing I did was sign up for skydiving lessons.

For the first 30 hours, I did tandem, which involved being strapped to somebody's back and jumping out of the plane with them. Once I was seasoned enough, I started doing my own jumps--you train, you pack your chute, you jump, use the altimeter, hit a certain height, and then you pull your rip cord.

In total, I ended up doing about 44 jumps there and another four here in Chicago. It was exhilarating to see the world from coming out of an airplane, being able to see the sky, the mountain range, and Spokane, Washington, which was near where we went to jump. It was amazing. I was addicted to that and skiing. When I went skiing at Whistler, I would take a helicopter service, they would take me to the backside of the Canadian Rockies, and I would ski down. It was an adrenaline rush.

MT. RAINIER–GOT THE T-SHIRT!

One of the other major things I checked off my bucket list during this time was climbing a major mountain in the world. Living so close to it, I climbed the summit of Mt. Rainier. I accomplished it through my involvement with the Seattle Mountaineers, and it was symbolic for me.

There was a whole training process you had to go through

before climbing. This was to condition your cardiovascular system for a higher elevation and the lack of oxygen and physical toll it takes due to exposure to the elements, harsh temperatures, and the sheer physical nature of the climb on Mt. Rainier.

With an elevation of over 14,000 feet, it is not an easy summit to do. In May, which is one of the times when climbs are done, the summit can reach lows of -6 degrees at night with piercing wind that chaps your exposed skin. Also, Mt. Rainier seems to have its own weather. There are storms that park at the top which even in the Spring can make a lot to contend with. The snow cap makes for cold nights and even with great gear, it's not for neophytes.

Aside from the sheer significance of it, one of my most vivid memories was the last day that I climbed Mt. Rainier. We broke camp under the cover of early morning darkness, and started the climb towards the peak on the Disappointment Cleaver route, and our guide, Garret Jannsen, had us stop as daylight was about to break.

There we were, mostly crawling on hands and knees, tethered to each other, wearing harnesses, and carrying lots of gear—pick-axes, headlamps, and crampons. The lower oxygen levels make every breath you take of the frigid air even more restricting. You feel as if your lungs freeze with the arctic air. The wind seems to pierce your balaklava, and the goggles you wear to keep your eyes from burning, keep fogging up. It's some of the most uncomfortable conditions you can dream up. You're hungry, cramping, thirsty, and just want a warm bed to curl up in.

Just as we were breaking the summit, the sun was coming up, Garrett called for us to stop and climbed up alongside our team of six to give us a speech, err, pep talk. "Many of you are probably cursing me under your frozen breath, but that is ok," he said. "Our current elevation is 13,825. Many people consider this a successful climb and many people at sea level might agree. Everything in your body is telling you to quit right now, your cramping legs, the churn in your bellies, perhaps your freezing fingers and toes. But you know what? We aren't stopping yet. We have roughly another four to five hours to go to get to our destination of 14,411 feet above sea level, and that is a successful climb. I want you to do one thing. Look over to the east. See that sun? It's going to make things a tad easier on you. I also want you to look down. In your quest for the summit, it is important that you acknowledge how far you have come, because it pushes you to climb higher, rise higher, and achieve more. After all, what are you doing this for?"

As Garret imparted his speech I thought, wow, this is so symbolic of where I'm at in life right now. I'm hunched over, tracking up, you can see the sun coming up, and you're tethered to the person below you and the person in front of you. I was thinking, man, this is impressive. If I could bottle this feeling up and take it with me, I'd be unstoppable. Perhaps it was the adrenaline rush, but it seemed like nothing could stop me, nothing could defeat me.

I was at the top of the world, and the sun was about to shine down on me. It was an amazing time in my life–I had made it through another breakup, I was sailing, had already raced across the Pacific three times, and I wasn't about to let any grass grow under my feet. Not one single blade. This is what it's all about–never looking back.

MOVING ON

My career then took me from Seattle to Miami and back to Chicago, where I was about to start my business, Karma Yacht Sales. I was taking a class on human empowerment and self-fulfillment, and one of the exercises in the class was to write letters to people from your past who did things that you felt hurt you in order to put closure on the matter, deal with it, and put it behind you.

While I had buried my head in work all those years, I knew that there was still pain inside. I came to terms with the things that had been hurting me–perceived injustices that I felt might have been limiting my personal progress–and I decided to be grateful for the fact that they happened to me. Those moments of pain and injustice are fundamental pieces of who I am as a person. Much like a steam locomotive uses combustion to drive itself, they served a purpose of driving me, fueling me. But the time had come to let them go.

As part of this exercise, I wrote a long letter to Janie, and then one of the next exercises in the class was to actually call the person in order to make sure we created a clearing, and then put it to rest. My letter said something along the lines of, I understand that our relationship wasn't going to work, and you did the mature thing at that point in our lives by calling off the wedding, even though there was the heartbreak of getting back together and then breaking up again.

At this point, I'm dating my wife, but I got together with Janie for lunch out in Rosemont. While we had lunch, she talked about all of our friends in college and how when we broke up, she lost all of our friends to me. Her part of completion was sharing that heartbreak, how she felt that was wrong, and I said, you know, decisions have consequences. We each lost something in breaking up.

So, I shared the stuff about her mom, and she told me how well I had turned out and how she might have been immature in her decision. I disagreed and told her no, quite the opposite, she had been mature enough to see the forest through the trees and say, this is not the person I want to be.

She added that if she'd been more patient, maybe it would have worked out. She had married Mark, the voicemail guy, and would later go through a divorce. She wondered out loud what would have happened if we had stayed together.

I remember telling her that I don't look at it that way because I've accomplished so much since we broke apart, and I don't know that I would have been able to accomplish that. Had we stuck together, would I have gone to Germany? Would I have climbed Mt. Rainier? Would I have crossed the ocean? There were so many things that came from that decision, that took me in many different directions.

When I look back on that period, and as devastating

as the pain was that I felt, I think it transformed me as a human being because it allowed me to stretch far outside my network, to think of who I was as a person, to cement my values, and then to go and never look back. When I talked to my wife about it, she said there are no regrets there because you did get back together, and it was not to be.

Now, when I talk to people going through a heartbreak, and they're wallowing in their pain, I want to grab them and hug them and tell them it's going to be OK. After the pain, it's going to be fun. That they're going to find 10 years from now that this was the best thing that ever happened to them, and they're going to want to thank that person for what they did.

That's how I felt towards Janie. I was very thankful—I couldn't have been more thankful in the letter that I wrote her, and I think she was shocked.

As I look back and then forward, I think of my family. I've got my wife and my daughters, and they're my life, they're my world. I thought, how am I going to coach my daughters the first time their heart is broken, because it's going to happen? Maybe that's why I'm trying to be as detailed in my story, because perhaps at some point, they can pick up this chapter and read it when they're in that wallow of hurt and pain that seems like the end of the world.

It might seem like the sun is never going to come up, but you know what? There I was on the top of Mt. Rainier, and the sun was shining. It does come up—every day. And one day, sooner than you expect, you'll see the sun shining and know it's for you, just as it was for me.

We are a compendium of our experiences, and we are also a compendium of how we react to those experiences, and it either propels us and drives us to the top, or we can wallow, spin out, and hit a low that we can never recover from. I believe it's about choices and not getting stuck. What do you want to be? What do you want your experience to be about?

Chapter 8:

COMFORTABLE WITH RISK

"You have to see failure as the beginning and the middle, but never entertain it as an end."

~ Jessica Herrin

The roots of my entrepreneurship began when I was little. At an early age, my parents encouraged me to take risks and not be afraid of failure, a large component of the credo held by many entrepreneurs.

It started with working on little projects with my dad. He would always begin by saying, "Hey, you know what?" It might have been out of shortness of patience or shortness of resources, but he would explain what we were going to do and then always said, "Go ahead and try it. If it doesn't work out, let me know what happened, and we'll figure out what you've learned from it."

The first time might have been when he was reroofing the garage, and my brother and I, just being boys, were constantly picking on each other. He was growing impatient with our childishness, and he finally said if we were going to continue to play with hammers, we would at least do some work with them. So, we were told to get up on the roof, and he started the lesson with, "Ok, you guys, this is how you do this."

Of course, it was then that I said I wanted to try doing it a different way. He never said no, it has to be my way. Instead, he would tell me to try it my way and let him know if it did or didn't work out. He always allowed us to do that, and if we didn't fail, which did happen, he would sit us down and ask, "So, what did you learn from it?" It took on a different meaning when we got older. In a way, in his own way he nurtured our comfort with risk, reward and failure.

LEARNING HOW TO FAIL SO I COULD SUCCEED

The experiences that my dad provided gave us the chance to test different things and allowed us to create and innovate. For me, it showed up in different ways. As a young kid, I would get an idea and run with it. At that time, kids could buy kits to sell magazines or Christmas cards or wreaths or different knick-knack items, and I remember deciding I wanted to make money, so I ordered a catalog of Christmas cards to sell door-to-door.

I would go from house to house on our block and sell

those Christmas cards. I probably got a whole seven or eight orders from the whole block. It was a massive failure and a big consumption of my time for very little return. I think I got maybe 25-50 cents per box ordered.

Later, we would resort to service-based ideas. Opportunity knocked with the great Blizzard of 1979, when a bunch of my friends and I decided to take our shovels and make some money. We had a lot of elderly residents that lived on our surrounding blocks, so we went to their houses first because the snow was just piling up. There were huge piles of snow everywhere. We provided a service and were paid handsomely for it.

As life might have it, we learned another whole lesson later when, after shoveling all day, my buddy and I got jumped by some kids who took all the money we had earned. We had planned to use that money to buy ice skates at a secondhand store.

I've tried to do the same thing with our daughters, to pay it forward and allow them to try things, too. I thought of my dad the day my daughter came to me during the pandemic and said, "Dad, I want to try this childcare business and I said alright, what are you going to charge?" She said, "I want to do it for free at first, to see if it works." It was her way of doing a test pilot, to see if she was able to get any families to trust her with that.

She did get a couple of families to let their children participate and we advised her to do it in the park or backyard where they would be out in the open since people were hesitant about being indoors due to Covid-19. Her next idea was to make and sell pumpkin dog treats, which began the conversation about cost of goods, profit, managing inventory and setting the sale price.

She had a chance to try both of these. She was able to get a few kids into her daycare but later abandoned the idea. Later, she baked up a bunch of pumpkin dog cookies, sold a few bags, and then fed most of them to our dog. The beauty is in the lesson of trying and learning.

GETTING TO KNOW CO-WORKERS
THROUGH SAILING

We've talked about how I started sailing when I was 10, and it started as an invitation. Then, later in life, when I began working at Abbott, it became a way to connect with people. I was now working in a Northern suburb with a lot of people that were unlike those I grew up with on the South Side of Chicago.

I didn't have a strong connection to a lot of the people I worked with, and everybody else seemed to know each other because they all lived in the northern suburbs or within close proximity to each other. So, there was a lot of hanging out after work, but because I lived in the city and was commuting, that didn't work for me.

Then, one day, one of the guys who was a sailor said, "Listen, we're getting together and sailing over at Waukegan Harbor. What kind of boats have you sailed?" I said, "All kinds of boats, but mostly J24's."

I brought a sailing bag, and one day after work, I met up with them. It was great; I didn't know anything about sailboat racing, but I knew the nomenclature of the parts of the boat since I had sailed as a kid. They showed me how to do the bow, and eventually, I worked my way into doing some jib trim, but a lot of it was self-taught.

This was a nice way to be included in some of the daily dialogue at the office because now I'd become part of the group they hung out with, and it became a way for me to build relationships.

That was the beginning of my ability to use sailing for a purpose to build and nurture relationships.

BUILDING RELATIONSHIPS IN SEATTLE

Eventually, my career transitioned, and I moved to Seattle. This was a blind move for me, without any friends or family. All I knew was that there were mountains and the ocean, which seemed like the best of both worlds. I needed to be near the water, so it checked that box, and I liked to ski, so it checked that box, too.

I moved to a place called Belltown, which was right by the Space Needle and an area that was becoming gentrified but still a bit on the bohemian side. The nice thing was I was close to Lake Union, and I loved to ride my bike. On one of those bike rides, I saw two people getting ready to go sailing, and I asked them how I could get involved with that.

I didn't know anyone, and I thought it might be an excellent way to meet people. At this point, the only people I knew were those I worked with and the customers I interacted with daily.

The couple told me to go to the Seattle Corinthian Yacht Club, so I went over there and asked how to get involved. They said, put your name on the board there, and somebody will call you. I put my name on the board, and a few days later, I got a call.

They asked what positions I had experience with, and I told them I had done bow and jib, although I hadn't driven much. They invited me to come out, so I started sailing with them and became part of the community.

As I got to know the people there, I discovered that a lot of the guys who sailed in that fleet applied their trade to boating as well. They might be technicians or other types of marine tradesmen—the one guy was a diesel technician, and another guy had a boat cleaning business that he ran out of the harbor.

Then, as I was going through my day job, trying to break the ice and build a rapport with the surgeons I was calling on, I would look around their office for something to talk about. I often noticed a picture of a boat or a model of a boat or some other marine paraphernalia in their office. It would become a focal point of conversation, a way to get them to talk about themselves and build rapport.

BIRTH OF THE SIDE HUSTLE

When I asked about the boat, they would open up and get into the conversation. I remember one doctor, specifically.

He was hard to get in to see, and the other reps said I would only have five minutes with him. While waiting in his office, I looked around and noticed a boat artifact.

When he rushed in and, in a gruff tone, said, "What have you got for me," I decided to take a different tack. I said, "It's an interesting boat barometer you have on your desk. Do you like boats?" Suddenly, his face lit up and he started telling me about it, and kept going on while I was getting nervous, thinking he would use my five minutes on the boat and then kick me out.

After 15 minutes, the nurse came to say the patients were backing up. He asked me if I could come back at 5:30 since he had used up all my time, and we would talk some more. The thing that was common about him and many of the people that I spoke to about their boats, is that they either had a boat, but they might not use it as much as they wanted to. Or, they might not have friends to go out and help them sail the boat or drive it if it was a powerboat.

It was an interesting phenomenon, and most of these guys had some nice 48 or 50-foot boats. They're very nice vessels, but they would say they didn't get a chance to use them enough, and that became a recurring theme. I started thinking back to a conversation I had with the guys after a Regatta. They said that happens a lot where people have boats but don't have the time to take care of them, and before you know it, they sell it, or it rots in the harbor.

It wasn't long before I floated a business idea before a couple of them that addressed their pain point of not being able to use their boat. I had identified four types of people--the person that has the boat and doesn't use it enough because he's short-handed; the person that would love to use it but doesn't have the time to provision it and get all the stuff ready; the guy that loved his boat but never had time to deal with maintenance; and then the guy that just wanted to show up and have everything taken care of.

I put together my pitch for them, and during one of these after-hour conversations, I asked a couple if we put together a service that addressed their problems, so the boat was ready to take out when they wanted to, with it all cleaned up, maintenance done, and supplies stocked in the fridge. Would they be willing to pay so much per foot for the service?

After getting positive responses, I started putting the boat management service together and named it Compass Boat Management. I decided to push all the business through the guys I'd gotten to know—they were my subcontractors–a diesel repair guy, a rigging specialist and jack-of-all-trades, a guy that had a cleaning business, and another guy who was a registered boat captain and could move the boats around.

I said, "Listen, I'm going to run all my volume through you guys. The only thing I'm going to ask is that we focus on the customer and make sure that if they ask us to do something, we under-promise and over-deliver. And there's no not showing up for work or not doing what you're supposed to do."

I did it all with a pager, a cell phone, a handwritten list, and a book of this stuff that we had to do. It was the bare minimum but viable and a nice side hustle that brought in revenue of about $4,200 a month for one of the boats and $5,400 a month for another one. The most I managed as a side hustle was six boats because something was always going wrong and needed repair.

When my career came to an end in Seattle, I sold the book of business to one of the guys I had been sailing with. He started his own company, took over all the customers, eventually rolled it up, and became a partner in a marine dealership in Seattle.

WE HAVE A BUSINESS MODEL

I moved to Miami and was given a territory that extended from Dade and Broward counties, all the way south to Key West. It was a large area with more responsibility, and I began sailing down there, too.

I was sailing out of Coconut Grove Sailing Club, and before you know it, I got a phone call from a doctor who knew about Compass Boat Management from one of his medical school colleagues, and asked if I would be interested in doing the same thing in Miami.

When I said that I wasn't doing that anymore and had sold the business, he said he would even give me the money to start it up. It wasn't about the money as it doesn't take much to start it up, but it's more about the market and getting reliable people to do the work.

Eventually, I did start the business. I wasn't able to manage as many boats in this marketplace because it was just a side hustle for me, but it made some nice side money that I was able to invest and use to create other opportunities. The bigger challenge in the Miami market was being able to find reliable labor. I remember, one guy showed up to clean a boat. He was so hungover from the night before that when the owner showed up the following day, the boat wasn't ready, and he passed out on the deck sleeping. I fired that guy.

Then I hired another guy who did tell me he had a drinking problem, but I chose to trust him. He ended up breaking into the liquor cabinet one night when he was on a bender and decided to throw a party on the boat and pass out. It was a mess and became a real hassle, but I pressed on.

I also had a silent investment in a cigar shop in Coconut Grove during this time. My money was at work there, but I wasn't active in the business. It was passive revenue that I was able to get a better return on than just having it in the bank—it was a diversification of my investments.

I ended up selling the boat management business when Abbott moved me back to Chicago. As I looked back over that time, the success in Seattle was great, and the one in Miami was so-so, but I made great side money. I ended up selling my interest in the cigar shop a few years later and did well there thanks to a boom in cigars during the 90s.

THE BUSINESS OF BUILDING COMPANIES

These experiences started to open my eyes to the possibility of working for myself and building my own business. It was my opportunity to test and try different things. I go back to the career aptitude test I took in high school that said I should probably be a mechanic or in construction. Perhaps it was a different type of construction, the kind you build with your head and not your hands—the business of building companies.

Later in life, I would have a chance to read a book called *Rich Dad, Poor Dad* by Robert Kiyosaki and Sharon Lechter. It spoke of the value of having a business interest that created wealth for you. Principles that I had applied from the values my dad taught me on risk taking and trying things. Most of all, the intrinsic value of creating something that lasts and creates opportunity.

Building businesses identified for me how being an entrepreneur is really about being a bit of an opportunist because you see the opportunity, and it's crystal clear. You see the vision of what it looks like in its end state, and you see the steps moving back into where you're currently at. You are able to envision the outcome you seek to achieve.

This also takes me back to my bucket list, and one of the things on it was to build a meaningful business. I didn't just do it once; I did it five times, plus an acquisition. More importantly, it's identified for me how risk friendly I am because what's the worst thing that can happen? Instead of being afraid to take that risk, it's like jumping out of an airplane, which I did 48 times. If I can do that, I can surely start a business.

In a way, this brought me full circle. As I sat in the moment after my dad passed, I thought about the impact he had on my life. He allowed us to take risks. He allowed us to fail--sometimes straight out fall flat on our face, scuff our knees, bust our teeth, whatever it was. And then he'd pick us up, dust us off and say, "Well, it looks like you're probably not going to do that again."

That is why I learned not to be afraid to risk it all, because when you are on your deathbed, you want to know that you left no stone unturned. You want to know that you lived your life to the fullest, and there's nothing that you can say, "What if..." about.

Chapter 9:

A NEW LEASE ON LIFE

"We don't even know how strong we are until we are forced to bring that hidden strength forward. In times of tragedy, of war, of necessity, people do amazing things. The human capacity for survival and renewal is awesome."

~ Isabel Allende

In the early 90s, my dad was working for U.S. Steel South Works, the largest steel operation in Chicago, a job he had held for a long time. I was still living in Seattle when the end came. It was April 10, 1992, when the site was padlocked, what was left of 18,000 jobs came to a screeching halt, and it was the end of an era.

It left a strong impression on me, how working for a

company over a lengthy period can become unstable because your destiny is in the hands of a lot of other people. When I started to look at that, I realized my dad was still at a working age, and he had relegated himself to doing stuff around the house. While he never said it, I could see the way that the situation with his employment and his ability to provide for his family and the fact that it was taken away, had crushed his dignity. However, my dad was a fighter.

Instead of becoming stuck in that role, he re-skilled himself, and this is what I was most proud of. He took the re-skilling opportunity they gave him at the union, went back to the community college, and got his GED because he never graduated from high school.

During that time, I would come home on vacation periodically, visiting with my family, and my dad had all these textbooks on the kitchen table. He'd say, "Hey, sit down, let me show you what we're learning." So, here's my dad sharing geometry, world history, algebra, and all the stuff that he was learning in his late fifties or early sixties, and for him, there was a real sense of pride.

I remember he would walk around, and he'd have a highlighter in one hand and a pencil in the other because he was always studying his workbooks, and he had such a sense of pride. It was great to see him really lit up with his education.

As I look back on that time now, I can see how he had lived vicariously through us, seeing us get educated, and he had put his back into work, making sure that his kids had a better future than he had. He had a chance to get a taste of that himself, which I thought was amazing.

During that time, my mom began working at a grocery store in the neighborhood to make ends meet. My dad's pension was paying out, but it wasn't fully vested. They were making do, but my sisters were still in high school.

They always lived very frugally, but it's a challenge when you lose the main breadwinner's salary. So that's also when we started to see the neighborhood change. Crime went up, gangs took root, and drugs went rampant. It was tough to see what my neighborhood was becoming, and I thought about how all of this was due to the threat of foreign steel.

That's the threat of globalization on American business, and for me, I saw the all-or-none approach that labor unions rendered on a lot of people. They pushed workers to the sidelines. While some might argue the union bosses were looking out for the workers' best interests and trying to keep their jobs, I saw those union leaders in their Cadillac Eldorado cars who had moved over to Gary, Indiana, and continued to work.

At the end of the day, the men and women that worked in the steel mills were left on the sidelines, and my community has never recovered. It led me to decide that I needed better control over my destiny because my dad didn't work that hard to create a future for us, only to put my future into somebody else's hands.

DISCOMFORT, GROWTH, AND PROMOTIONS

As I was going through the evolution of my career at Abbott, I was still in Seattle and earned a promotion. I was putting all my effort into my career, checking off some bucket list items, and while things were good at that time, I was also wondering where it would lead.

Would I get a shot at coming back to the home office? That's where the disconnect for many people of color happened in corporate America. There are very few of us at the top, and seldom are there role models or, more importantly, sponsors that will help us get to the next level-- people who advocate for us in the room where the decisions are being made. Someone to say, hey, Lou is doing a great job in Seattle.

My boss in Seattle was Felix Liu. Felix was the guy who hired me after the 45 interviews and 45 no's. He was a tough guy, to the point where it was excruciatingly painful sometimes. I had to over-deliver and prove myself, but the great thing about Felix was that I always knew in that discomfort I was growing. I knew that being able to over-perform created an opportunity to be promoted, and, eventually, I went to Miami.

In Miami, my manager was Jeannie Maguire, and she also became a very good mentor. If you performed, she made sure that she got your name in front of the right people so you would get promoted. She would say if you've got talent and you're still working for me in a year, then there's something wrong with both of us.

She embodied what being a sponsor should be, and that is who I try to be for people who I mentor. She inspired me because she had come through challenges in her life and career as a woman rising through the corporate ranks. I learned a lot from her, and she created many opportunities to make sure she highlighted her team's strengths.

I also learned a lot of my operating principles from her. Teamwork needs to be there, you need to be collaborative as a leader, you have to create camaraderie on your team, you need to have transparency as a leader, and be able to take input and feedback from various directions. She also showed us you need to have integrity as a leader, do what you say you're going to do, and then under-promise and over-deliver.

More importantly, she taught me that you need to celebrate your victory. Jeannie was good at celebrating those victories, and we had a lot of victories. We had a high-performing team in our region, and she made sure that everybody got highlighted for their hard work. She was my inspiration early on in my corporate life.

Then, I moved back to Chicago, the home office, and got caught up in that whole corporate thing. I became very disenfranchised because now I was back in the corporate bucket. I didn't have a mentor or sponsor like Jeannie, and I started looking for my next move.

THE BIOTECH CORVETTE

I'd had a fair amount of success, but then it became one of those things where I thought, there's got to be more. So,

I followed another mentor, a guy who had left the company and went to Bristol Myers Squibb. I followed him to become a regional account manager.

I learned a different skill set, and Bristol-Myers is a great company, but I felt unfulfilled. I was given more responsibilities there and had a great manager, Kate Greble, who embodied a lot of the same things Jeannie had--teamwork, collaboration, camaraderie, transparency, integrity, and celebrating your victories.

That common theme cemented for me the foundation of who I've become as a leader. Probably the toughest decisions that I had to make came when I was with Bristol Myers, and a call came from a headhunter with an opportunity at Alza Pharmaceuticals. They were a biotech startup in Palo Alto, California. Compared to my experience at Bristol Myers and Abbott, which are very large, billion-dollar companies, it was a small company. This move put me in what I would best describe as the Corvette of the biotech world.

This company made decisions in a flash. As a leadership team, they set my goal to hire 300 reps in 120 days, so you roll up your sleeves, and you get to work creating your region. That gave me my first taste of what being at a smaller organization and being in control of your destiny was all about. They heavily incentivized everybody with stock options, so being brought into the start-up company, you got a very big equity stake in the company. As you might imagine, as one of the first series of employees in the company, I got in at the ground level.

I went all in, and we created our region. It was a good feeling to create something from the ground up, start with a lump of clay, and mold a high-performing team that I hand-picked to do that. For me, that was the epitome of my career in terms of being a leader.

It was more inspiring for me and more fulfilling to create things from the ground up, which gave me a taste of it all. I had already had the taste of doing the side businesses in Seattle and Miami, which were like startups, and the cigar shop in Miami, an acquired business that let me start creating a cash flow I could invest in something.

I was a year and a half into my time at Alza, and we'd done really well. Suddenly, we got an announcement that we were going to be purchased by a very small company called Johnson & Johnson. I couldn't help but wonder, what did that mean for me? What it meant financially for me were a lot of great things. The deal was transformational for many of us, it represented a $10.5 billion dollar acquisition with complete vesting of shares and paralleled equity in J&J stock.

It was clear, though, that J&J had bought the company for the products and less so for the people or anything we had built. They are a good company, and they do well by their employees. Still, you get plugged into an organization and being the outsider--the acquiree--there's often a perception of how you went about your business. Sometimes it's founded, and sometimes it's not.

There was a lot of criticism of how we did things, how we

grew the business, and to be realistic, everybody knew that they would merge us at some point. That's generally not employee-friendly.

NEW BOAT, NEW FRIENDS

At that point, I had been back in Chicago for about five years. I had already bought my first boat with my brother, my friend, Jake, who would become my business partner, and his brother. We bought our boat for $7,200 and did a lot of sailing on that little boat named Chiquita. It was an appropriately-named yellow sailboat of 1978 vintage with an ugly, Brady Bunch brown plaid interior. On the boat, the name was the Chiquita banana logo with the city of Chicago in it.

That was my first opportunity to get on the water in a boat of my own. A lot of great friendships were bonded over cigars and beer on that boat. There came a point where we were putting as much into the boat annually as it was worth, so we decided to sell it, get ahead of the depreciation curve, and buy a new boat.

We looked at all the different boats and eventually decided on a 2000 model year, 33-foot Beneteau. During that process, I got a chance to meet the owners and develop a friendship.

My corporate life was still evolving at that point. It was 2001, and I was in Chicago, renting a spare bedroom to my friend, Jake, who had recently broken up with his fiancé. In addition to being roommates, we played hockey together, sailed the boat together, and had a lot of common crossovers in our lives.

Jake was also at a point in his career where he was becoming very disenfranchised. He was a district manager for a record store chain, with the traditional retail grind of managing employees, pilferage, and going into work and having to cover for absentee employees because he was the boss. He was a good individual from an operations perspective.

NEW BUSINESS?

In the meantime, my career trajectory had worked out well for me, and then Joseph and Elaine Darby, who sold us the boat, invited me to start working boat shows on the weekends. During that time, I developed a strong friendship with them, and they were teasing about wanting to sell the business.

They were an older couple running the business out of their basement on the Southwest Side of Chicago and had a 25 percent market share with an old-school way of running things--no automation, no processes, nothing.

During my experience with them, I found it interesting that they seemed to do everything they could to not sell us the boat, including not returning my phone calls and not meeting me when I wanted to see the boat. It was almost comical, and I remember thinking it shouldn't be this hard to buy a boat. I thought if they could have a 25 percent market share and do everything to prevent business from occurring, what would happen if you modernized it? What would happen if you just focused on the customer and created an enjoyable buying experience?

I started talking to them about selling the business, and they expressed interest. Then, in a parallel fashion, Jake and I were having conversations, and he was talking about how he didn't want to retire from a big business and wanted to go into business for himself.

I had already discussed the financials of the company with the Darby's. So, I brought him into it. Jake and I had already talked a couple of times about doing other businesses together and, at one point, looked at the viability of owning an ice rink, a bar, or a hockey shop. Still, we ended up going into boat sales.

I passively invested in it. Jack quit his job completely and started working in the meat of the business in 2001. While we were negotiating the sale of the business, Jake was learning the business from the inside out, and I continued my day job and worked in Karma Yacht Sales on nights and weekends.

At the same time, things had changed at J&J now that Alza was a fully owned part of the company. We were placed in the Ortho-McNeill division and my region had been resized. The dynamicism of the Alza days were gone and we were now BIG Pharma. The opportunity to take a package and exit the company with all my shares intact came up and I jumped on it. I already had my exit ramp picked.

I resigned, vested my options, took my parachute, dedicated myself to Karma, and that's when the business started thriving. That was my first taste of being in control of my destiny.

Of course, I then was approached by some people to do consulting back in my old line of business, biotech, and accepted a retainer to do consulting for them. It allowed me to monetize the intellectual capital that I had acquired in my biotech and healthcare training. I created a consulting company named Hippocratic Health Solutions and we were off! Now I was juggling two balls, and it was very engaging for me to do that. It really stoked my creative, building nature and I was learning tons.

This structure allowed me to continue building Karma while making money on the side consulting gig that I spent 15 hours a week doing. I had gone cold turkey into Karma in 2003, about a year-and-a-half after the start of the business. We paid off the owner's financing after two years, and I started taking a modest salary.

Looking back over that period, I could see the writing on the wall--that I needed to go into business for myself. The high school career assessment had said I should work with my hands, and while it might not be working on cars or building houses, I was building a business, and that's what I think I was put on this planet to do.

PUTTING LIFE INTO PERSPECTIVE

In 1998, I had just gone to work at Bristol Myers Squibb,

and I went to the doctor for a routine physical. The doctor asked the usual questions, and one of them was whether I'd been experiencing anything unusual. I mentioned that I'd been having night sweats, to the point where I would wake up, and my undershirt would be soaking wet.

He said, let's check it out and then ordered blood tests. He got the results and ordered more testing, and when those results came back, he asked me to come back to the office for another appointment.

I got to his office, and once I was in an exam room, the doctor came in and said he had good and bad news. I told him to give me the bad news first, and I would just deal with it. So, he told me that the blood test came back, and I had indolent B cell lymphoma, a type of non-Hodgkin's lymphoma (NHL).

I remember looking at him and thinking, what does that mean? That's when he gave me the "better" news, saying that it was treatable with radiation therapy and removal of my affected lymph node, but the bad news was that I had cancer. He explained that we might be able to put it into remission after three months of radiation therapy. Loosely speaking, I might be able to live a normal life. There are a lot of studies, but since it is a slow growing cancer, it could be placed into remission. With regular check-ups, I could live to be an old man.

This was the last thing in a series of events that led me to think about what I wanted to do with my life because life is too short. And I remember how I kept it from my parents because I didn't want them to know—I was carrying this cross, and it was mine to bear at the time. I couldn't help but to think of Bobby Mularsky from Boy Scouts. This must have been how he felt. Bobby was a smallish sized Scout in Troop 750. He didn't take too well to summer camp and would cry from homesickness. He attended camp one summer with us at Owasippe and later dropped out of Scouts.

That Fall, we got the bad news that Bobby had been diagnosed with late-stage Leukemia and died. Attending his funeral was surreal. Seeing someone of your age in the casket is hard to take. That whole camp session, we all seemed to be invincible and then Bobby was gone. Why did God do these things? Why did I get this test? Was my fate to be like Bobby's?

I would go every other week for the radiation therapy, and I learned that the good thing about this type of NHL is once they radiate your lymph node and consequently your long bones, your immune system can get stronger and it turns against the cancer cells and kills them.

The challenge is that it could pop up with a recurrence at any point. Infections, stress–you know, the usual stuff. There are theories about cancer, that when you're going through periods of stress, your body takes that stress and puts it in a variety of different forms. Then, there are the random bad luck moments, like Bobby's. Why?

What I always ask myself is, all the stuff I'm doing at work, all the stress, is it now costing me what I value the most? I remember praying and talking to God and saying, "Hey, if this is my time to go, then I guess I'm okay, but I'll tell you what. If you let me get through this, I promise I will not complain—ever—for anything that I've got to carry on in my life."

After the third month of radiation therapy, there's a cooling period, and then you go back for blood tests and PET scans. When I came back for the results, the doctor told me that my white cell count was good, I had stabilized, and I was in remission. Big thanks to God, I made it. Even now, though, I have to be careful because stress could bring it back.

That challenged me to think about what I wanted to do and needed to do. That's why, when the issue came up with J&J and the unhappy situation, I thought about how I had a choice, and I definitely didn't need the stress. Life's too short, and I was going to keep my promise to the big guy that I would not ever complain or look back, but I would take it for a learning experience and move on.

Once I got over that, I eventually got back to good health, but there was still a lack of fulfillment on a personal level. I still hadn't found somebody I wanted to spend my life with, and I was looking for her. I think every guy goes through this, and women do as well.

Jake and I became roommates right after this, and we were both doing a lot of philosophizing in our lives. We were in our mid-30s, engaging in a new business venture, had gone through break-ups, were commiserating with each other, building a friendship, and smoking cigars, which probably didn't help, but it was one of those things where life wasn't guaranteed.

That whole experience made me think about tenacity and what has happened during my life. It made me look at my life from the inside out and ask, what do I want to see? What should be different? What was I put on this planet for? So, I went back to my bucket list to see what was left to do. As Mr. Capello said, leave no regrets on your deathbed. Time to get to work.

CHAPTER 10:

FINDING MY PURPOSE

"The two most important days in life are the day you are born and the day you find out why."

~ Mark Twain

After working in Big Pharma, moving to a small startup is like taking a race car out on the track and running the fastest laps you've ever imagined. It's exhilarating, it's freeing, and no one is going to hold you back.

Going to work for Alza Pharmaceuticals was that race car-liberating because not only was I more than just a number, but it also allowed me to create something. Sure, helping to build a 600-person salesforce means you're putting in a lot of long hours, but it's also an everyday adventure with a lot of positive reinforcement. You are learning, you are challenged, you are uncomfortable, but that is totally part of the experience. You are growing, by leaps and bounds.

As I wandered back to my bucket list and evaluated where I was versus where I wanted to be, I was finding my professional life rewarding, but on the personal side, I still wasn't finding fulfillment.

While I dated a lot, there was still a lack of meaningful relationships. I had dated one lady, but then she moved to London, and while we tried long-distance dating for a bit, it became obvious it wasn't worth pursuing–we weren't a match, because we weren't aligned.

I was doing a lot of traveling for work, leaving on Sunday, coming back on Friday, and living out of a suitcase. The nice thing is that my region went from Chicago to Colorado. So, I could leave a pair of skis and golf clubs in my employee's garage in Colorado. That way, if I wanted to boondoggle on the weekend, I could go skiing in the winter or play golf in the summer months, and it was a lot of fun.

MAKING A DIFFERENCE

Even though I was getting what I'll call intrinsic internal fulfillment, I began to realize that I needed to get back to some of the things that mattered in my life. So, I started volunteering for Big Brothers Big Sisters. I was assigned a young man named Onofre who lived right behind Farragut High School.

He was a big kid for his age, about 6' and in eighth grade going into freshman year of high school--a big kid, but gentle, with a very soft heart. His presence was intimidating because of his size, but he was a child at heart. Getting to know him was interesting. There were parts of him that reminded me of myself, what I might have been had I not been given the male role models I was blessed with (minus the size of course).

His mother worked at a laundromat at the end of their block. His sisters were raising him alongside his younger brother. So Onofre was the oldest male in his house because his father was serving time downstate for crimes he committed. I did a lot of interacting with his counselors at school, and they were trying to put together a plan that kept him out of trouble.

I developed a working relationship with his mom, too. We were mentoring Onofre as a team. When his mom was worried, she'd reach out to me and tell me about things he was going through. It was a challenging time, and I could see a little bit of what I might have become if I hadn't had the influences in my life that kept me from it.

He came from good values and a working-class family, but faced other challenges because he was undocumented. That meant if he was to get into trouble, it could cause bigger issues for him, and his mother was sensitive to that. I spent a lot of time talking to her. My job was to help him stay out of trouble and give him somebody to talk to.

I found it unique that even though he only lived a block from the pink line, he had never been on a train. So, one of the first things we did was take the L downtown. I left my car in front of his house, and we walked right down the block to the pink line, got on the train, and it was amazing seeing the world through his eyes.

Those few blocks to the train, though, were treacherous because there were several gang factions, and you couldn't go through there without them trying to recruit you. He was isolated because a block north was one gang, and a block south, there was a different gang. And then the other dichotomy was that his house was in the shadows of 26th and California, which is the lockup.

They weren't giving him what he needed to become educated. He wasn't being stimulated, so we did a lot of talking about why education was important. I tried to instill some of the values that I had growing up, but obviously, I'm working with a kid who is 13 years old, and a lot of the formative values have been put in place already. That did not deter me. I did not quit; I went at it with the same tenacity that only I know how to deliver.

There was only so much that I could do other than have conversations with him, and the troubling part was that even though he had no interest in joining the gangs, he was being heavily recruited and his sense of awareness was that he needed to be the one who gave in.

He reasoned that it was better that he joined instead of his younger brother. He said, "If I don't go into the gangs, they're going to go after my brother, and I don't want them to recruit him." So, he saw himself as a sacrificial lamb, and I told him it didn't have to be that way.

It was easy for me to say, of course, because I wasn't living his day-to-day life. It reminded me a lot of what could have happened to me if I didn't have the mentors that I had. I remember taking Onofre sailing with an old friend, showing him the world, and introducing him to my friends who are Caucasian. He had a lot of resentment towards Caucasians because his entire life in the Little Village neighborhood, it had been portrayed to him that white people were bad.

You know, it was sort of an indoctrination. He met my business partner, and he met other friends that we had on the crew, and he would say things like, "Wow, they're actually pretty nice. I always thought white people were bad. That's all we were told in school, that white people were bad."

This is the downside of not having diversity because, in his community, there was no diversity. It was mostly Hispanic and black with few teachers who looked like the students. While that has changed much since that period, it continues to be a challenge for youth of color. Representation matters because you may only aspire to be what you see others becoming.

GIVING BACK TO MY ALMA MATER

I also decided to give back to my alma mater, DePaul University. DePaul is interesting because of its position as a university in a major urban center. It allows a lot of working-class students and 1st generation college students to work and still attend classes at night.

I decided to volunteer with the DePaul University Hispanic Alumni Association. Part of our mantra was to create a conduit for Hispanic students to see themselves beyond education. There was a bridge program that allowed kids who might not have the ACT score to get into college, to sharpen the skills they needed to be successful in college. That program mostly served the African American and Hispanic communities.

Students would take that program in the summer after high school and then enter DePaul University in the fall, and the rewarding part was seeing those kids come in and flourish. Getting to school was part of the problem but staying in school was the hardest part. When we started tracking enrollment and engagement, and retention, the first-year numbers were great.

They were starting to get a student population in the low 20 percentile range, but the second-year population dropped dramatically. That is because it's during the sophomore year when family pressure, commuting challenges, financial pressure, or going to school and working at the same time really hit home.

A lot of times, students had to provide for their families because their parents didn't have full-time employment. And the Latino culture of "everybody pitches in" would sometimes force them to decide between their education and dropping out to work full time.

We tried to serve as mentors for those students, to encourage them to stick with their education because if they could get past their sophomore year, the data showed that they would stay with it and graduate. There would be a huge drop off after sophomore year, and most of that was due to disengagement, finances, or struggling with classes.

I found my involvement with both volunteer opportunities to be rewarding outside of my career. Sometimes, if all you're focusing on is your career, and you're not giving back, it can leave you with a hollow feeling. Giving back was also the way I was raised.

THE FATEFUL NIGHT

I had been on a long run of Sunday to Friday back-to-back weeks where my schedule consisted of going to the airport on Sunday, flying to whatever city, getting ready to travel, and driving from one city to another. Then I would return home on a Friday night flight, go to the dry cleaners on Saturday, and exchange clothes before starting the whole cycle again the next day. Rinse, wash and repeat.

I didn't have much of a life. What little bit of life I did have, I was putting into those other organizations and mentoring Onofre.

I would arrange my schedule to participate in things when I came home. We had been planning a couple of different alumni gatherings, and one would take place over on Erie Street at a Tapas Restaurant. My vice chair Alana and I had coordinated this event, and we had a lot of people planning to come.

She called me mid-week to confirm that I was going to

be there, and I said, "Well, I'm in Denver right now. I'll get in about 6:30 on Friday, but I'm exhausted, and I need to go home and relax." She wasn't too happy with my response and said I had to go because I was the chairman, I had to give the opening statements and some gift cards for door prizes, and then I could do whatever I wanted.

I didn't want to be there, but I went anyway because she had a good point. After I was done, I had a little something to eat and talked to a few people when I saw this lady on the other side of the room.

She was pretty and had a nice smile, was wearing a blue suit, and looked like a real baller and shot caller, so I decided to talk to her and ask what her name was. Her name was Sonia. When I asked where she lived, she said the Southwest Side of Chicago, and I said, "Well, that's funny, I grew up on the Southeast Side. So, you were a Sawaseda (sah-wah-sayda)."

She asked me what I meant by that, and I told her that's what they call girls from the Southwest Side. She gave it right back to me and said, "Whatever. You know what they call people from the Southeast Side? Stuck up." The Tapas restaurant part of the evening went well, so I got a second wind and a group of us went on to an Irish bar, Apres. I asked Sonia to go, but she stiff-armed me and said no. Strike one. That first encounter didn't go very well, but I got her number and email address, so we had a point to start on.

A SAILING EXCURSION TURNED DATE

On weekends I would go sailing and coordinate alumni events for different groups of people to go out on the lake. I added Sonia to my email list of invitees from the DePaul Alumni Association. One day in early June, I suggested we get together as a group to go sailing, explained what to bring, and that boat food protocol meant they should only bring finger food and nothing greasy, slimy, or red.

Everybody agreed to go out Saturday morning, so I got the formal invite out on Monday. Then, on Thursday cancellations start rolling in, and more came on Friday. By Saturday morning, I lost track of who was coming and who wasn't, but I knew some people were coming, so I went down early and started cleaning the boat.

As I am into the scrubbing of the boat, I see this young lady walking down the dock with a case of beer. I took a quick look at the list of people on my phone, and most had canceled. I was dirty because I'd been cleaning the boat, and when she came up, I said, "You're the first one to come up, and hopefully you're not the last one, but I'm not sure who else is coming. It could end up you and me and one or two others, if that's ok with you.

In the meantime, we got another cancellation, and it turned out it would be only the two of us. I asked if she still wanted to go, and she asked if we could handle the boat with only two people. I said I could do it all, so we backed the boat up, took it out, and went sailing for about five or six hours.

During that time, we had a couple of drinks and talked about life. I shared with her all the different things that I had been focusing on lately--mentoring the young man through Big Brothers Big Sisters, why I was mentoring this young man, and the volunteer work I was doing with DePaul University.

If you ask my wife now, Sonia will tell you that was probably the moment that did it for her because she was starting to see me differently. I had stopped being this stuck-up guy in a suit and became more of a person with a heart. It was nice to be seen that way.

That was the start of our future together, and later that night, we met up with a bunch of the others at Bluesfest, which happened to be that weekend. Later, Sonia told me a friend was having a graduation party, so we went and time went by fast until we suddenly realized it was close to three in the morning.

It had been a great day together, and I told Sonia I'd love to see her again. She pointed out that I had her number, and I could give her a call. After a few more dates, I asked her if she wanted to be exclusive.

She said, "Let me think about it." My reaction was to tell her it was either a yes or a no; there's no thinking about it. I'm very decisive about things, and that's probably something that she likes and probably dislikes to this day.

The insight for me, is that when I stopped caring about finding the "right one" and just focused on being me and the things that mattered beyond myself, magic happened. It was the start of Sonia and I.

AN ENGAGEMENT OF THE RING KIND

A year later, almost to the day, we got engaged.

We had already talked about what we wanted our wedding to be like and where we would get married. Sonia could see that we aligned completely on family values, how we wanted our future and family to be, that we focused on education, how we wanted to raise our kids, and what we wanted to build together.

Everything from that point on was more of a matter of us getting things in alignment, and then one day, she came to me with a positive pregnancy test. I think she wondered, what was this guy going to do? She had a difficult family situation, and at that point, her dad was in jail, serving time for a DUI.

Her dad had a drinking problem, and her parents divorced because of it. For me, there was the aspect of trying to be there for someone who had grown up with alcoholism, and that can be challenging because it creates a lot of mistrust and other issues during their formative years.

A lot of this happened when she was in her early teens, and I thought, wow, this is a lot to handle, but I still cared for her deeply, and I loved her. So, when we got the positive pregnancy test, at first, I thought to myself, now what are we going to do? My next thought was there's only one way forward—we'll get married.

So, we talked about it; I told my parents and she told her parents. They were less than happy about the situation. There was no mention of marriage at that point to the parents, just that I was going to do right by her. Complicating the matter was the fact that Sonia and I have almost a thirteen-year age difference.

This happened about eight months into our relationship. And then she had a miscarriage, but that didn't change things in my eyes. My path was set. I still wanted to get married to her, and we had this opportunity to go on vacation to Mexico and get away from all that had just happened.

We had such big families on both sides, and I didn't want an expensive wedding. We talked about a destination wedding and thought Riviera Maya would be perfect. Sonia had been drawn to that area because when she had done her Spanish immersion for DePaul, she had gone there to learn Spanish and stayed with her friend Karla.

So, we went on vacation to check it out beforehand, and I decided that asking her to marry me there was cheesy, so I waited until the weekend after we got back. I took the time to talk to her mother and her stepfather, and I said, "I want to ask for your daughter's hand in marriage."

Her mom said that was ok, and then her stepfather said, although he will deny it, "She's pretty cranky in the morning, so you better get used to that." One thing was for sure, he was on the anti-deal-making team.

One of our favorite places to take walks was on the corner of North Avenue Beach, overlooking the Drake, the old Playboy tower, and that whole area of downtown. I had a camera and tripod on me, and I said I had to take some pictures against the lakefront for business. At this point, I already had the dealership so it was a good alibi.

I asked her if she could help me get some pictures of the skyline. It was just a ruse. I had the ring in my pocket, in a little cloth bag. I asked her to walk away from me to see what the view was like from that vantage point, and while she did that, I put the bag with the ring in it on the sand. As she walked back, she stepped on it and buried it in the sand.

So, I said, "Hey, why don't you go back over there and try it again. As she turned around and walked back over, she didn't step on the ring again. So, I took it, shook it off, and put it back on the sand while she was fussing with the camera to take a photo.

I said, "Did you see this? What's this bag here?" She walks back and says, "I don't know; what is it?" I suggested she open it and look to see what that is. So, she picks up the bag and feels it, thinking it was drugs or something. Then she opens it and says somebody lost a ring. I said it looks like it was meant to be there as I got down on my knee and asked her to marry me.

She was kind of shocked and said yes, but it was like pulling teeth to get it to happen.

We held our wedding a year later at an all-inclusive resort after taking one more trip down to plan everything and get it all lined up. What we thought would be a small event ended up with almost 80 family and friends joining us.

The wedding wasn't without its challenges, thanks to a

wedding planner who left a lot undone. We were lucky we went down a week ahead and could get everything squared away. We had picked the flowers already, so that part was done, and her dress was already there because we had brought it with us from Chicago. So, it was just a matter of a few details that needed to be taken care of.

We had planned to go down early, let the planner do her thing, and have some fun since Sonia had started scuba diving lessons and had completed all the classroom work in Chicago. I signed her up for the open water certification at the resort, which was like boot camp every morning.

As it turned out, the whole wedding party was there early, and between scuba diving and spending time with the wedding party, it helped to keep the stress level down for Sonia due to distraction.

We had fun with a lot of the family, completed her open water certification, and then it was our wedding day. Everything went off masterfully. Sonia had been stressed over the big day and even debated delaying the wedding until her dad was released from jail so he could walk her down the aisle.

As a result, I made the unpopular call to go ahead and not wait. We didn't know at the time when that would happen, and I didn't want it to be put on hold forever. A bit more of my decisiveness. It turned out that a few years later, he got out on good behavior, but it was a bumpy ride during that period of planning the wedding and all. The wedding itself was a blast. With all of our family and friends there, the evening was wonderful.

We have a lot of memories of trying to take pictures at the Tulum ruins and getting chased by the guards because they didn't want you to take pictures next to the ruins unless you had a commercial permit. The photographer got his cameras snatched from him, and my wife got in the middle of the whole thing and wanted to knock the security guard out. More proof that you just don't mess with a girl from the Southwest Side.

Right about now, if I wanted to get real cheesy, I could say that it was a fairytale wedding, but the fact is it was great. Without forcing the issue, I had accomplished one more thing on my bucket list–finding the person that I wanted to spend the rest of my life with. More proof that when you stop chasing the dream, the dream finds you. It always does, and eventually you find your purpose.

CHAPTER 11:

FATHERHOOD

*"The first time you hold your child in your hands,
you know that your world is forever changed and
they will be your sole responsibility–for your entire
lifetime." ~ Lou Sandoval*

My dad instilled a lot of values in us. We used to call it *tu palabra*, which is *your word*, and it means being committed to what you set out to do, and making sure you see things through to the end.

One of the biggest things that dad taught us was his work ethic. And it was something that we all grew to admire. We used to say he was like the post office—he went to work in the rain, sleet, snow, no matter what. Growing up, I remember he never missed a day's work because if he felt sick or was ill, he would go anyway. Nothing was going to keep him down.

The classic episode with the birthday cake and strawberry filling–the allergies, the reaction, and going to work anyway–was just one of many instances of how he did not miss.

We always knew that he had a dangerous job, especially later on in high school, when we became aware of a classmate whose parent had passed away on the job. One guy's dad had been killed when he fell into one of those giant vats of molten metal and died instantly. Another person's dad was run over by a train. There were all these trains moving cars full of metal and different raw materials, and the train driver didn't see him.

So, the fact that he would go in there with his eyes swollen, and the dangers he faced at work, showed his commitment. For all the things that he had to deal with, we understood that he knew he had bigger responsibilities--and that was his family at home.

There was one other occasion when we were in high school, and he was injured because one of his fellow train operators showed up to work hungover, as it was determined later. They used to have these big cranes with large steel girders, and they would move the beam and load them on the flatbeds of other trains to transport them. I guess my dad ducked to get out of the way, and as he was dodging, the steel beam caught his forearm, ripped through his work clothes, and tore a big gash in his arm that required 30 stitches.

He still wanted to go to work the next day after having

left the hospital, but the union rules around those accidents dictated that there was a cooling period. Because it was a workplace mishap, they had to investigate the situation, and that involved a mandatory drug and alcohol test to make sure that there weren't any illicit substances. My dad was suspended without pay for three days because of this accident, although he was eventually vindicated. While his test came back negative, the coworker's came back positive.

That spoke to my dad's commitment to what he set out to do, what he was building, and his dedication and loyalty to his family, to make sure that we were always provided for. That meant he just worked a lot. Every four days, he'd be on a different shift, so he would rotate from mornings to afternoons, and then nights with four days on and then one day off.

He worked a ton, but the plus side of that is that we never wanted for anything. We always had food on the table. There was always a roof over our heads despite our parents having tough financial times later in life. No matter what happened, they never showed it to us.

The downside is that he missed a lot of things—little league games, baseball games, hockey games, football games, and a ton of camping trips—stuff that you do with your kids. We had some great family vacations, but those were usually planned in advance. Being a silly kid and not knowing any better, I would resent the fact that I never had my dad there at those things, and I told myself that if I ever got to be a dad, I would be different. I would be present for my kids.

BECOMING A FATHER

I vividly remember the day that I found out that I was going to be a dad. It was a Sunday morning, and Sonia shared the EPT test with me. I was beside myself with happiness. I was finally going to be a dad! It was also one more thing on my bucket list, but it was less about that. It was very welcome after having had the miscarriage many years prior, and we definitely felt it was a blessing.

We knew because of the miscarriage that we wouldn't be out of the woods until the first trimester was over. There are statistics say that if you that if have one miscarriage, there's a chance you might have a second. You just don't know.

So, months later, when we had the ultrasound, we found out the baby was going to be okay, and that was great. We also decided to wait until birth to find out if we were having a boy or a girl. I think Sonia was convinced the day she saw the ultrasound that she would have a boy. So, the journey through the pregnancy was an interesting one for us both because somebody had a lot of cravings for Chinese food.

I had nine months to prepare to be a dad. I took a lot of time to think about what kind of dad I wanted to be, taking the things that I learned from my dad, too. I spent a lot of time with my dad during that period as well because we were in the process of moving from my place in Wicker Park to a house we bought in Bridgeport.

We moved in there in April of 2006, and Sofia was born in November. Sonia was quite pregnant by the time we moved down there, and then we had to get the house in order and get everything straightened out and ready to go. There have been a lot of opportunities to spend time with my dad since he retired. He would come down to help, and I remember doing a lot of painting with him, talking, and trying to take in tips about what it would be like to be a dad, what I should be looking forward to, or maybe not looking forward to as much.

Then, on November 26th of 2006, Sonia's water broke in the morning. We were nervous first-time parents and called our parents to say our "son's" water broke, and we would be heading to the hospital. We had already set someone up to walk our dog at the park, so we got to the hospital late that morning, went through the check-in process at the hospital, and Sonia was dead set against having an epidural. She insisted that she would do this naturally, and the poor thing went through about 10 hours of labor.

You're wiser the second time around. In hindsight, we realized we probably didn't have to go right away because she wasn't fully dilated just yet, but you hear all these stories that if the water breaks and you don't get there in time, you can have all kinds of complications. So, we got there, and we spent a long time waiting. Sofia wasn't born until close to 10 p.m., and we had gotten there at close to 10 in the morning.

While Sonia was pushing, I had the Bears game on and a nice view of the lake. I'm sitting there, watching the Bears game and listening to my wife push because she didn't want anything to do with me. As we got further into the whole thing, I remember her continually asking, can she change her mind—can she get the epidural now?

It was too late for that, but she was getting tired. Imagine 10 hours of labor—she was beat. In the end, I think they threatened her with a C-section if she couldn't have the baby naturally. They were worried the baby had the umbilical cord wrapped around her neck because the heart rate would drop during contractions.

My heart was racing as I saw the baby coming. The first thing I saw was a purple baby and the umbilical cord around her neck. The doctors worked their miracle, and she started crying. I breathed a sigh of relief, and then was hit with the magnitude of what it's like to be a dad, a parent, when I held her in my hands for the first time.

I was hit with the impact that my world was changed forever–in that instant it became reality.

That was the birth of our first daughter, Sofia Isabel Sandoval. We picked Sofia because we loved the name, and because it also meant wisdom. That, for us, was everything–it manifested who she was to become.

As I had taken the time while Sonia was still pregnant to think about what kind of dad I wanted to be, I also thought about how I want to be different? Then, I'm watching this little girl grow up, and I'm starting to think a lot about the world around us. I'm looking at all these different things that are happening.

MAKING A DIFFERENCE THROUGH SCOUTING, AS AN ADULT

Sonia had some challenges in her family, with little boys

kind of going the wrong way. Her nephews had gotten wrapped up in things they shouldn't have been involved in. I thought about what kind of world I want for my daughter. I started thinking about it, and I started looking at the biggest challenge that I think a lot of parents had--trying to raise those kids from when they were five until they turned 14 or 15.

That's when some kids can go off the rails, and I thought back to the people that had an impact on me growing up. I decided to write a letter to the CEO of the local Boy Scout Council that I had grown up in. I asked to get involved, and it blossomed from there. They brought me onto the Board of Directors, and I was charged with leading the Hispanic initiative for the council, which was taking scouting to the Hispanic community and trying to help get more kids involved.

Prior to that, I had been involved in Big Brothers, Big Sisters. This was the next step in giving back a bit of what I had gotten out of scouting. I spent almost a decade in scouting as a leader and on the council board. I was on the local council and on the national council. At some point, I was appointed to be the vice president of the council (Council Commissioner) and I led a four-council merger, bringing four councils together into one to help the council survive. I was involved during a very tenuous period in Boy Scout history–the acceptance of the LGBTQ community and having scouting be more open and diverse.

We laid the groundwork for what eventually became the opening of Boy Scouts of America to little girls. I really got a chance to do a lot of interesting things. This was happening while my daughters were young, so they were going with me to a lot of different things. They went on camping trips, and they got to see scouting through my eyes and what I liked about it.

They learned to fish at a very early age, they were their own cooks when they were four or five years old, and they got a chance to go camping and to Boy Scout camps. Later, when they started to go to Girl Scouts, they compared the two and said, how come Girl Scouts teach us to do baking and cooking, and Boy Scouts learn how to do rifle shooting and fishing and all kinds of other stuff? That was the stuff that they liked to do.

HONORING FAMILY NAMES

When Sofia was born, she was given my grandmother's middle name, Isabel, to become Sofia Isabel Sandoval. When our second daughter, Sarah, was born in 2008, we gave her Louise for the middle name because it was unlikely we were going to have a son. The funny joke in the family is that we got stuck on one letter of the alphabet because we have a Sofia, we have a Sarah, and then my wife's name is Sonia.

We named Sarah with an H after the biblical wife of Abraham from the Old Testament. In Hebrew, it means princess, and in Arabic, it means joy. As our second child and the youngest of the house, I can truly say that she has lived up to being the joy of the house. She is an intricate combination of drive, spunk, and can do. Nothing stops her. I wonder where she gets that from?

With the birth of our second daughter, and living in a house with all women, I think that cemented the fact that I am paying for whatever I did in my youth (I like to kid around.)

I tell my buddies that I remember at one point in my life— it must have been some time in college—that I must have sent a prayer to God. And I said, "Jesus, please, I want to be surrounded by beautiful women." God has a way of giving you what you need, not necessarily what you want, and you need to be very specific because as I turn around now, I'm surrounded by beautiful women. It wasn't quite what I had in mind at the time, but I did get the blessing.

UNDERSTANDING MY DAD

When I look back at the last 15 years of being a father, I had one of those moments when, for the first time in my life, I truly understood what my dad was about. You know, going to work even when sick, putting your kids before yourself, because from the minute they're born, you want everything for them. You want the best for them. You want them not to suffer the way you might have or to have met certain challenges.

Even today, we tell our daughters, "I know it sounds like we're ragging on you. I know it sounds like we're trying to tell you what to do with your life. Just understand that it's because we've made those mistakes, and we want the best for you—to learn from our mistakes, so you don't have to experience them yourself."

I remember my dad telling me, if you keep doing that, it's not going to end too well for you, or whatever message he was trying to get through to us at the time. And we were always saying, yeah, yeah, yeah, whatever, dad. You don't get it until you become a parent. That is when you truly understand what they meant all those years ago.

I suppose that is why I struggle to understand parents who are absent in their kids' lives. Because for me, from the first moment that I saw my daughters, I realized that they came first–before me, and sometimes even my wife. We put them first, and I think it has a lot to do with the way you're raised.

You want them to have things that you might not have had a shot at. I have nothing to hold against my dad--he was a wonderful father—but I had early on committed that I was going to be different, and I was going to do things with them. I was going to seek a career and job where I could take time out, and I was very blessed because, for most of their upbringing, I had my business. In a way, because of mom and dad's sacrifices, I have been blessed with the opportunity to make those choices.

I had the flexibility of being able to, when they got sick at school, bring them into the office and have daddy daycare in the conference room, where they could play with cardboard boxes, packing peanuts, and bubble wrap. They could play office or stuff envelopes or whatever they decided to do that day, but they were with me, and we had our own special memories that we created out of that. Memories that I will cherish for a lifetime.

DOING IT DIFFERENTLY

I think every generation thinks of that in their own way, about the things that they didn't like growing up and then decide I'm going to do it differently, whatever that is. For us, that included a lot of neat things—the ability to go and be present at their school fairs, plays, pageants, all the things in the middle of the day that I know my dad couldn't do because he worked a shift job that didn't give him that flexibility.

I think the blessing to me was, even though I was pursuing my dream of having my own business, it gave me the flexibility to do things that I needed to do and needed to provide for my family. Sure, it was challenging at times during the recession and everything. However, flexibility is something that is invaluable.

I remember the day that my wife lost her job during the recession. She had just gone back to work after maternity leave from Sarah's birth and had been back for about three months. At first, they cut back everyone's hours, and then they told her she was getting laid off. So, we pulled both girls out of daycare and decided to tighten things up a little bit to make it work.

Sonia was home for a few years until she went back in 2011. It had been tough because my business wasn't doing well during the recession, but at least it gave us the flexibility of having one parent home during that time.

I remember during the depths of the recession–there were some dark days for the business. Looking back on it, I can see that everything happens for a reason, even though at the time we were going through it, I thought, "Man, this is really brutal." But we persevered, we made it through, and realized there were a lot of things we learned about ourselves, especially that we are stronger together. The kids got the best of both of us, and while we weren't rolling in dough, we were getting by, and it let us focus on the things that were most important, which is, I think, the way my dad would've wanted it, the way our parents taught us to focus on the things that were most important.

DO YOU HAVE REGRETS?

I remember after we moved, my dad was helping me put up sheetrock in the garage. We had put the insulation up, we were done Sheetrocking, and then we were taping the seams so we could finish the job and paint it. My dad helped me sheetrock, tape the seams, and sand. And then, the next weekend, Sonia's dad came over.

When I was a kid, the walls in our house were plaster and lath. I remember when they tore wallpaper off in our bedroom, it took off a lot of the plaster, down to the lath boards beneath. So, my dad actually replastered it, and I remember him working little by little, one hour at a time because he would work his shift, come home, work on it for one of the six hours he was off, go to bed, then get up and start all over.

As we were remembering that, my dad looked at me and said, "Yeah, this is a lot easier than when we were doing the plaster in the old house. I wished I had the money to be able to buy drywall and just do it this way, but I had tuitions to pay."

I asked if he had any regrets about that, and he was firm, saying absolutely not. As I look back at that time in our lives, I still remember when my parents went to the hospital to meet Sofi for the first time. My dad was so proud of his grandchild, and he already had a bunch before that. Sofi was the eighth grandchild, and my kids were the last two of the nine. We call them the last batch.

Being the oldest, I did my life in reverse. I lived it and then had a family. So, when my dad said, "I have absolutely no regrets at all," he added, "Because I think the way it worked out is the way it worked out. You've now found your way, you've got your family, and you got to do things the way you wanted." I thought that was a cool thing for him to say.

When I'd ask him for advice, Dad would say, "Listen, I'm not gonna give you advice on how to raise your family. Just do it the best way you can, because there is no book, there is no way of doing it. You just do what you think is the best. It's all about making decisions. It's all about making those decisions with the best information that you have in front of you."

YOU CAN BE ANYTHING

When Sofi was born, it was amazing to be able to look down at this tiny baby that fit in a third of my arm. It was a sense of wonderment that this beautiful little being came out of my wife. This little girl who we saw grew up in ultrasounds and pictures for nine months, and now here she is.

I wouldn't have done it any other way. Early on, we were tempted to find out the gender of the baby, but we decided to wait and be surprised. Sonia was convinced she was going to have a boy, down to her cravings and everything.

But, when I held Sofi, that's really where everything comes full circle. You realize in that one second that your life's never going to be the same. You have fundamentally made one of the biggest impacts that you can make on the planet. But it's only just starting because it's not just having the child that's important, but even more, it's what that child becomes. That they grow up with a good education, that they grow up with values that allow them to be productive members of society, and to accomplish what their potential is. You see that little being in your hands, and you look at them, and you think, wow, this little girl can be anything she wants to be. Anything.

We're all born with that, and I thought from the time Sarah was born, and now we have two girls. My job is to open up as big a door as possible for them. Now, I'm a dad of just daughters, or as I like to say, a Dodo, a dad of daughters only.

There are no gender stereotypes here at this house. The girls got hot wheels and a lot of toys where people might say, "Hey, why are, why are your kids getting boy toys?" We intentionally never taught them gender stereotypes with toys. They played with hot wheels, they learned to fish, and they played baseball.

This weekend we celebrated Sofi's 15th birthday, and to this day, I continually tell the girls, I don't ever want you to think that you need a man to complete you. You are whole, you are complete, and you are capable of anything you want to be. If you decide at some point in life that you want to partner with somebody, then that person should contribute to you. It should be additive because you should hold your own for what you are, make your own money, and make your own rules.

Much has been written about parenthood and the profound impact that it has when you are blessed with the single most important job you will ever have in your lifetime, being a dad. Beyond that, there are a variety of highs and lows. I won't lie–it is challenging at times. You do stand committed to your responsibilities as a parent, focused on near term goals with an eye on the future. There is no guidebook. You operate by gut, intuition, prior experiences, and you do the best that you can for a lifetime as you will always be their father.

CHAPTER 12:

DREAMS BECOME REALITY WHEN YOU ARE OPEN TO POSSIBILITIES

"Most people miss great opportunities because of their misperception of time. Don't wait! The time will never be just right." ~ ***Stephen C. Hogan***

Living the dream is different from one person to the next. For me, it began with a little seed of an experience when I was a Boy Scout in a small sailboat on a big lake. It gave me a feeling and freedom I would never forget, and over the years, that little seed germinated and grew, helping me through all stages of life.

The dream began moving quickly after I moved back to Chicago in 1997. I bought into a boat partnership with my business partner, Jake, his brother, Paul, and my brother, Marty. Paul and Marty already owned a little Venture 21 together, which I had sailed on with them when visiting. It needed major repairs, so they decided to buy a different boat and thought it would be a good idea to take on two new partners.

The new boat was a 1978 AMF Paceship that we named Chiquita because it was yellow. It cost $7,800 and we took out a note for it. It was ugly, with a Brady Bunch interior that was a brown plaid that we later reupholstered. But we were four bachelors with no responsibilities, and it was just fine for us.

We all knew each other from high school. Jake had graduated in the class of 1982, I graduated in 1983, and Paul and Marty graduated in 1985. Not only did we know each other well and had played sports together, but our families knew each other well.

The first summer we owned it was wonderful. Our logbook showed us sailing 52 adventures which, of course, included a lot of cigars, beer, and parties. We threw a lot of parties on the boat, so it was quite the merging of all our different worlds. A boat is an opportunity to create a community with a group of friends around it. It was a load of fun.

Over time, we began spending more and more on repairs for the boat. And even though we tried to do it efficiently, it was starting to cost a lot, and every year it kept creeping up. I think the first year, we probably put $4,000 or $5,000 into it. That's half the value of the boat right there.

The next year I think we were somewhere in the area of $5,000 or $6,000, and that's when we started considering the purchase of a new boat because the repairs were going beyond the value of the boat, and we wouldn't get that back in value-added to the boat.

We decided our next boat should be something a little bigger, and because we didn't want someone else's problems, we decided to buy a new boat. We began researching boats and came upon the brand Beneteau. We saw tons of them in the harbor; they were everywhere.

BUYING KARMA

Beneteau is a French brand that was locally represented by an eccentric and cute little old couple in their early 70s, who worked out of their house in the Southwest Side of Chicago. They kept their stock at a boatyard named Crowley's over on Corbett Street in the Bridgeport neighborhood, which, ironically, is the area I moved to later.

As we started researching the brand, we discovered that Beneteau had a good following and great presence in the local market. In what one might call a happy coincidence, we had been storing our yellow boat, Chiquita, at the same yard. We were looking to trade her in on a new one, and we happened to see a boat with a Darfin Yachts for sale sign on it.

So, we called the number, and I took the lead on it. I got

a voicemail and left a message saying we'd like to see this boat you've got here at the yard. Is it available for sale? And all I got were crickets. A week goes by. Two weeks go by, and still no return call. I called again and left another voicemail, asking if it was for sale or not.

Finally, I was talking to people in the yard where the boat was and was asking who is this Darfin person? They say it's that old guy over there with the fisherman's hat, the guy who just putts around in the yard.

So, I went over to him and introduced myself. His name is Joe Darby, an Irish gentleman who is very affable. I said I was interested in the boat and had left a couple of messages for him. So, he says, let's go look at it.

I asked him what the boat cost, and he talked around it but didn't give me a number, so I asked if he would send me something on the price, and he said yeah, he would. Another week goes by, and still, nothing. Now, I'm used to car dealers that are all over you when you want to buy, so this has me saying, "What the heck?! Does he want to sell us a boat or not?"

He had given me his cell phone number—he has this old Motorola flip-phone—and he has a hearing aid. I said, "Joe, it's Lou Sandoval. We met a week and a half ago about the 33 you had in the yard."

He comes back with a yeah, yeah, yeah, how you doing? I don't think he remembered me right away, but I reminded him he was supposed to get back to me with a price on the boat, so he asked me to meet him at his office on the Southwest Side of Chicago.

I get out there, and there is no water anywhere near it. I see this house and think, "Am I in the right place?" I called him to be sure and described where I was, in front of this house next to a yard with a bunch of old boats in it.

He said I was in the right place, and then I saw him coming out a side door from the basement. We go in, I sit down, and he goes to get me a drink. His wife, Elaine, was there, too. She's obviously the business manager, very endearing, and together they're a quaint couple.

We hit it off, and while talking, it became clear that he would break into fits of stories, but you couldn't get a straight answer from him on anything. I finally got back to the price of the boat, and he said, "Elaine, can you bring over that folder on the 33?" So, she milled around in the back, and God knows what she was doing, but after about a half-hour, she brought it out. Joe asked if I wanted a cocktail, and I said I would have a beer with him. I had to smile when Elaine came back with Hamm's beer for us.

Joe opened the file and said the boat was $63,000. We began going through a whole song and dance of, is it for sale? How soon can you deliver it? What does it come with? He said it comes with everything, and we'll put the electronics on there, too.

He told Elaine to type up the quote, which she did—on a typewriter, old school style. So, I asked if this price was final, and his scattergun approach to negotiating is to pretend he didn't hear you. I told him that I wanted to know if that price had any wiggle room in it and asked if taxes were included.

He came back saying it was a fully commissioned boat and kind of droned on for a minute, so I said I needed to think about it. Elaine went in back to make a copy using some very loud machine that made clunking noises.

I walked out with the quote and couldn't help but think about how surreal that whole experience had been. When I got home, I called everyone, and we met over a beer— not Hamm's this time. This process began in the winter, but now Joe is hot on my trail, calling to ask if I'd met with my partners and inviting me to come out to his office-house again.

That first meeting took three hours just to get the quote, and I can't help but think this guy was a waste of time. Now, I would have to clear my schedule because this was probably going to be an all-night event.

I got to his place, and we went through the Hamm's beer ritual again before getting down to the details. I had negotiating power from Jake, my brother, Marty, and another partner, Rob, a good friend from college. If they agreed to a certain price and answered some questions, we would be in, but I wanted to get the best price from them first before introducing the concept of trading in the old boat.

He said the price was $68,000, and I told him we would pay $65,000. After he and Elaine went in back to talk it over, we agreed on $67,000, and I told him we needed to talk about trading in Chiquita. Joe suggested selling it for us, but we had all agreed that we didn't want to own two boats.

So, Elaine brought out all these big books, the various used boat pricing guides. He was looking through them, asking what kind of boat it was, and then started telling me stories again. Joe was amazingly full of stories.

As we got to know them better, I realized this was partly their tactics, and partly just the way they were. They were kind of cagey and older individuals that were somewhat mistrusting. They were kind of funny like that, but we continued to negotiate and ended up meeting halfway on the trade-in price, and he said, "Let me take a look at it. Maybe we could meet in the yard." At this point, we are four hours into the meeting, and now we've agreed to another one.

This process has now taken close to two months. We began in January, and now we're talking March or April, and I wanted to have this boat ready for the start of the season. I told Joe we were all good for the boat, and he came back to ask about financing.

I told him not to worry about it, that we were done and ready. We've all got good jobs. We've all got great credit ratings—we're good.

I agreed to meet him at the boatyard, so I got there, and Joe was known for driving these big Cadillacs, the land yachts. I was at the old Crowley's yard, slotted between the train tracks and the river. You had to go under a viaduct to get there. It's the only way you get in.

I pulled in, and I was waiting by our boat, which was right up the front. I had my ladder set up, and I'd been waiting half an hour when I decided he probably forgot about me, so I called his phone, and it just rang. So, I called the home number, and Elaine picked up. I told her I was supposed to meet Joe, and he hadn't shown up.

She said she would try him on his cell phone and call me back. I stood there thinking, "It shouldn't be this hard to buy a boat." After all, it's a pretty simple transaction—I give you a lot of money, and I get a plastic object. I go sail the plastic object with a smile on my face.

By this time, I've invested probably two months and 12 hours into this whole adventure. I stop musing about this process when I see a huge car coming from the other side of the yard, and I can't believe it. Was he over there the entire time I was waiting?

He asked if I wanted to see the boat, and I reminded him we were there for him to look at my boat for the trade-in. He went to park the car and came trudging back. I later found out that he was at the other end of the yards and just lost track of time. That was Joe, and Elaine was like his conscience, calendar book, and alarm clock all in one.

Now, I'm ready to take care of business and ask him, "So, you want to take a look at the boat?" He doesn't even go inside. He walks around it and pulls out this form. We tallied it all up, and he asked when we wanted to close. I told him as soon as possible because we were getting to the start of the season. He had to paint the bottom and get it rigged because it had come straight from the manufacturer.

Joe said he would have it ready on or about April 1st, and

we signed the deal that day for the boat we would name Karma. He suggested we could go back to the office and have a beer, but I passed on it that time. I realized that what I signed wasn't a formal contract, and I asked if we needed to sign one. He said yes, we could meet at the house-office again.

I said they would need to have the contract ready to sign when I came because, twice bitten, three times shy, and I would be signing on behalf of my partners. I had no intention of falling prey to another three-hour visit. I didn't have any more time to invest in it, and I felt like I had become their new best friend.

FROM FRIEND AND PARTNER TO ROOMMATE

On the other hand, there was Jake, who really was one of my close friends. We had become good friends during high school when we played hockey together. He had gone through a tough time recently when he and his fiancé broke up. They had bought a house together, and later when he learn about her have had a romantic entanglement with someone else during their engagement, he left her with the house and moved out.

He needed a place to stay, and I had the townhouse with plenty of space. I had a dog and an extra bedroom, and I offered to let him stay there for low rent—basically beer money for me. The next thing you know, I cleared all the stuff out of one of the bedrooms, and he moved in.

It quickly became a refuge from what he'd been through and a place to come home from his job and hang out. He worked retail as a manager for a national record chain retailer, something that was disrupted by the move to online music and streaming.

Jake was the middle child between two older sisters, a younger sister, and his brother, Paul. Jake didn't push too hard, so his parents told him he needed to go to community college, which he did before transferring to Western Michigan University.

While we lived together, I got to know him better--who he was as a person and what drove him. He is generally a really good guy. We became very good friends, and we'd go and hang out at the bars, go sailing, and play hockey on the same team. It was the start of a fruitful business partnership.

WORKING THE BOAT SHOWS

In my blossoming relationship with the Darby's, things seemed to evolve in a rather timely fashion. When one day Joe suggested, "Why don't you come out and work some boat shows? You're pretty good with people. I'll pay a commission on whatever you sell." I started with the Chicago Boat Show at the end of Navy Pier, and then I also went out to Michigan City, Waukegan, and a couple of others.

The Darby's were like an older eccentric aunt and uncle. You love them, but can't quite figure them out. As I got to know them, Joe would opine about "someday," and you could see they were getting on in years. Both were becoming forgetful.

They had three service guys, Jose, Chano, and Renee, who were Mexican immigrants. Elaine wouldn't call them by their names. She'd say let me call the Mexicans. It made me think, "Do I not look Mexican? Do you think I wouldn't find that offensive?" It made me think twice, like, who am I doing business with?

The day we took delivery of our boat, it was put in the water at the riverfront. We had asked for somebody to help us take the boat down and do an orientation. Then my boat partners showed up and were starting to ask, what kind of deal did you strike here?

So, I called Elaine because by now I knew that you couldn't rely on Joe to answer his phone. I reminded her that we had talked about somebody being here to go down the river with us because we'd never used this boat before. She said I'll call you back, and I thought here we go, another three hours.

She called back in about 10 minutes and said, "Bob's going to be there." Later I found out they had forgotten about it. So, they called up some guy who used to help them occasionally, and he also happened to be a priest. We used to call him Father Bob because he had really nice, long hair and kind of looked like a hippy.

Father Bob shows up, and he's like, "Hey guys, what's happening?" We told him we were taking the boat to

Millennium Harbor. We had been in Monroe Harbor on the mooring balls when we had Chiquita but put in a transfer and upgraded to a 40' slip in this newer harbor.

NEW BOAT, SCARY PROBLEM

We got underway and had gone through two bridges when all of a sudden, the boat started smoking, and it seemed to be low on antifreeze and overheating. So, Bob calls Jose, who starts running down possible problems as I checked them off, saying no, that's fine, nope, not that, and so on.

Finally, Bob says, ok, let's check that. He goes back, flips something, and—boom!—all of a sudden, water starts coming out. Mind you, we had never owned a boat with an inboard motor and we just assumed that the dealer would take care of that upon commissioning.

It turns out that the boat didn't have the raw water intake open.

I had jumped off at a drop and ran to a shop on land to get a fresh gallon of coolant.

After all that running, I was hot and sweaty. Once they told me the problem, we replaced the antifreeze that had burned off. After all that drama, it was clearly something that could have been prevented by proper commissioning and customer onboarding. Note to self, an opportunity for improvement.

Going through all the bridges in the middle of downtown

is stressful enough as it is, and then with a new boat and this happening, yeah, that sucked. It was not the way I envisioned our first day of new boat ownership would go.

NEW BOAT, NEW BUSINESS VENTURE?

While I was selling boats with the Darby's, I found out that they were thinking of selling the business. When I asked how much they were asking for it, Joe retreated with his usual stalling tactics of, "Well, I don't know... We'll talk about it."

At this time, in early 2000, I was still working at Bristol Meyers and later left to join this new start-up to create a new sales force. I asked him again how much he wanted for the business, and he said, ballpark of $250,000-$300,000. As a sign of progress, he made me sign nondisclosure and confidentiality agreements before revealing his financials.

After I got the big fat folder of financials, because none of it was digital, combined with what I'd learned about their way of doing business, I could see how they had a broken process. They could have been selling so many boats if they knew how to treat customers the right way!

As I started digging into the business, I found out they had a 25 percent market share in their territory against some very formidable brands. That was depressing because they were one of the original five dealers to bring Beneteau to the United States, and in 10 years, they had amassed a 25 percent market share. Imagine what they could have done if they dealt with people the right way.

I saw so much opportunity with this business. If the buying

and delivery process was a lot more pleasant, whoever owned it would be close to unstoppable. I'll admit that I'm a bit of an opportunist, and I knew this business could definitely be improved by the right process, fewer customer surprises, and a lot less Hamm's beer.

So, I came home one day, and I had just gone through the financials after having a couple of different meetings with Joe and Elaine—again, three or four-hour meetings— to talk about buying the business, and I figured it's a nice side investment for me. At the time, we decided to move forward with it. There had just been the announcement about the acquisition of Alza by J&J, and I knew where that merger and acquisition model was going to go. They were either going to buy us solely for the products, or partially the products and the people, and then eventually do away with the people that they don't want.

I knew that at whatever point an offer came, I would be ready and prepared with my life raft.

Rule number one, and being a sailor I knew this well, do not walk out of a perfectly good ship. I had a lot of shares in Alza as one of the original set of employees, and things were going to go pretty well for me with this acquisition if I played it well. I've always been a little bit of an entrepreneur, and I couldn't help but think that buying the business from the Darby's was a good opportunity.

MORE THAN A BOAT NAME

While we were waiting for the boat to be delivered, Jack

and I started talking about what to name it. Our old boat, named Chiquita, had a been a riff on the banana company logo with the Chicago skyline instead of a banana.

We started sailing the 33-footer, and had done our first Mackinac Island race as a team on the 33-footer, which was an experience in itself. Now, we're into the racing part of things, and this 33-foot boat wasn't really that fast. It was a nice boat with a nice interior, and we were probably going to do something with it that it wasn't equipped to do, meaning race fast. It's nice for cruising but not great for racing.

We're full-on into the sport. We're loving it, so, when an opportunity to buy the business came up, Jake and I would talk about it, and he would talk about how he hated his job. He hated being in retail and dealing with employees that always called off and everything that comes with managing a retail establishment.

We had already talked about opening an ice arena or a hockey shop. Or, maybe a bar, because 30-something single guys like hanging at the bars. It was good for my liver that the bar didn't happen, but we were both in this interesting, self-discovery period.

It was during this time that Jack and I took a legal pad and a case of beer and started scribbling down any names we could think of for the boat. At one point, we thought of horns on one side of the boat and a halo on the other—good karma and bad karma—and then decided that would be tempting fate just a bit too much, so we decided to name it Karma.

It wasn't long after that we started pursuing buying the

Darby's business. I still had a good job, but the business couldn't support us both. Now, we were going into this process of buying the business and thought, what should we name it? We wanted to create another entity altogether. We would start DBA as Darfin Yachts and then eventually phase the name out because their reputation—as we had experienced—was not the best, and their customer experience was horrible.

They were a very nice old couple, but they were not the best at dealing with their customers. They avoided them more often than not, as they had done to us. They didn't answer calls and just let the situation drag on. So, we eventually phased the name out and formed an LLC called Karma Yacht Sales. Our business philosophy was, "KARMA The Belief that Waves of Good Fortune Follow Admirable Actions."

In the end, we had named the new boat, which would soon become the name of the business that we were destined to purchase.

Throughout much of this journey, there were many things that I would probably change about how we went about it, but that's the beauty of the rearview mirror. Knowing then what I know today, but you don't have the luxury of that insight. Life unfolds as we live it. I strongly believe that what presented the opportunity of Karma Yacht Sales was a series of events that led to the purchase of the boat. There was no definitive action, rather a series of decisions. The beauty of looking back at this period is that we were open to the possibility and when one is open—the universe answers your call. Rather, opportunities present themselves. It is ours to decide whether we act or pass.

CHAPTER 13:

MANIFESTING THE DREAM-KARMA YACHT SALES

*"Fun is one of the most important–and underrated–ingredients in any successful venture. If you're not having fun, then it's probably time to call it quits and try something else." ~ **Richard Branson***

Sometimes life takes odd twists and turns that take you someplace you hadn't imagined, but when you look back, you can't picture it any other way. Even if things didn't go quite as you'd planned, there is always good that comes out of it and lessons learned that help you later in life.

That's especially true of Karma Yacht Sales. It was a challenge, it fulfilled a dream, and it broke a valued friendship. But before we get into that, let's go back to Joe and Elaine Darby, the owners of Darfin Yachts. We had bought a boat from them and, along the way, built a relationship with them. That evolved into working with them at trade shows, easing into a friendship, and then I found out they were interested in selling the business.

At that point, I began meeting with them, signed a non-disclosure agreement, and then they opened up their financials. I started looking into the business, coming up with a valuation for the business, and played the first hand of poker with Joe. He came at me and wanted to get half a million out of the business. I told him I just didn't see it in the financials, based on the historic revenue, the market, and immediate projections, so there was a lot of back-and-forth negotiation.

I told him I wanted to give him a fair price, but it had to be validated. I had to do that based on the valuation of the business after looking at the books and the revenue cycle.

FROM ROOMMATE TO BUSINESS PARTNER

So, I really dug into their financials and was pretty far down the road when one day I came home, and Jack was sitting on the couch. We were already roommates at this point, and he was having a beer and watching a ball game. He told me, "Man, I had the worst day."

I said he looked like death, and he went on to tell me how he was sick of his job and going through the retail grind. Working retail isn't always all that fun. You're working with people, dealing with a lot of returns and employee situations. As a store manager, you're the chief cook and bottle washer, and a lot of times, you're dealing with minimum wage employees who sometimes have a great work ethic, and sometimes they don't.

Jake was pretty good with people, and I think he cared a lot about his employees, but you have to deal with the nuances of that. And I think more of what was taxing him was having to deal with management, with the leadership of the company, and all the politics that come with that.

Then, truth be told, I think he was making a meager salary for someone with his skills and time out of school. It wasn't much for all the responsibilities he had, and they kept wanting to push more on him. So, he started asking, where's this going? And being a forward-looking person, he started to see the disruption that CDs were creating for vinyl, and then, you're in the early 2000s, so you're already starting to see the disruption of MP3 players fueled by Napster's streaming music disruption which was in full swing.

Looming in the horizon was this small thing called Apple Music with its iPod player that was poised to completely turn the music industry and bricks and mortar retailers on their head. This created a lot of concern for many in the retail music industry, and it signaled a very unstable future for all involved. In spite of the perks of promotional concert tickets, the work lifestyle wasn't all that great–working variable shifts, working all the time, and working weekends. Jake was burnt out and needed a change.

We had already had several conversations about potentially buying a couple of different businesses. We talked about building a hockey rink, but that didn't pan out. We looked at starting a hockey shop or sports business, but it didn't have the legs. I don't think it lit us up. And then, we had talked about buying a bar because there were a couple of bars around where I lived in Wicker Park that were for sale. But it's a tough business. It's a mostly cash business, you've got to be in it all the time, and the lifestyle is just so-so.

So, I said, "Alright, I'll let you in." I would see if we could extend the non-disclosure, and I suggested we go meet with Joe and Elaine. I was able to share the broad strokes of the business, but until he was added to the NDA, I couldn't go further.

I asked him if that was something he might want to do, and he said, let's see. So, we looked at it, we analyzed the numbers, and we put a business plan together. We talked to Joe and Elaine—several three-hour meetings with Hamm's beer involved.

We discussed pricing, and then we went to one of the shows at Annapolis and met with the leadership of Beneteau. We eventually got their blessing, and they wanted us to see the factory, to get to know the process and learn more about the product and how it was made. So, we went out there and met with them. We ended up working at a deal with a fellow hockey player and friend of ours, as our attorney, representing us in the matter and drafting our partnership agreements.

There was a lot of goodwill between Jake and me, and I believe we went into it saying that we would have equal sweat equity. The plan was for Jake to leave his job and go work for Joe and Elaine, and he agreed, saying that would probably work out best. He could learn the inside outs of the operations of the business. He was more operations oriented while I was more skilled at leadership, sales, marketing, market analysis, forecasting, and the like.

So, he quit his job and started working with Elaine as a salesperson and office manager. Jack had some success selling boats for them while they still owned the business during this interim period, and they paid him a commission on those.

STALLING THE SALE

One year turned into the next, and then, all of a sudden, 9/11 hit, and then Joe and Elaine were afraid of what would happen and began stalling and delaying, saying we'll sell it in the spring. We would have three-hour meetings—with Hamm's beer again--and you wouldn't get anything out of that meeting. Meanwhile, Jake's still selling, and they're benefiting from it.

The model year for Beneteau ends in June, you start selling new products on July 1st, and close out the previous year's fiscal year in September. We said we wanted to take the reins in 2001, and they said they weren't ready. You might argue that they were looking to improve the sales revenue pipeline to validate the price they wanted for the business. We started this process in late 2000, and it dragged on, so we said that on January 1st, 2002, we would take over. They complained that it was mid-cycle and unfair. But during that time, another problem surfaced. Jack had sold a few boats for the Darby's, and they reneged on the commission for them.

Jake and I regrouped and talked about what the potential was out of this. We could blow the deal up, and everybody goes their own way. Jake goes to look for another job, and I hadn't left my job yet. I was still working for Alza, which was being bought by J&J. We talked through it, and I asked, do we bite the bullet, look at the long-term picture, and say, let's even this out in the future somehow? In the end, we agreed, due to goodwill and in an attempt to keep it fair, that we would draw up a 50/50 partnership agreement of equal equity even though my financial portfolio was supporting much of the business financing we needed to operate the business.

On paper and in the bank, we had significantly different net worth. In our desire to get the deal done, we overlooked that fact and looked at the business as equal owners. It was a rough start for Jake from the beginning. I think, if it could be done over, I probably would've equitized it a little differently because later in the business, I ended up putting more money into it.

When we started looking at the business deal with the

Darby's more closely, it told us a lot about who we were negotiating with at the other side of the table. Their reneging on Jake's commission left a bitter taste. So did some of the comments that Joe and Elaine would make about "The Mexicans." They were a nice couple, but at the same time, they were very distrusting of the world and very old school about their money. A viewpoint that was a relic of older times.

They were very good poker players who didn't tell you much. They operated in their own way and weren't as straightforward as they should be. Obviously, that was one of the reasons why their business didn't flourish as well as it should have.

RUNNING A BUSINESS WITH INTEGRITY

Jake and I had a completely different way of operating, and that was we do what we say we're going to do. We act with integrity, and we honor our commitments. That didn't seem to be Joe and Elaine's way of doing things.

I think that galvanized Jake and me, that we were clearly in a values alignment where Joe and Elaine weren't. Even though we loved them, and they were great people, we knew we had to keep men at arm's length, and once the business was done, we wanted very little to do with them.

We created Karma Yacht Sales as a shell company, as an LLC, and then Karma Yacht Sales is the one that bought Darfin Yachts. We operated under a DBA for a period of a year and finally closed the deal on September 30th, 2002.

We opened our doors and moved everything out of the Darby's basement to 1945 South Halsted. It was an odd space and our office was a converted Catholic school gym balcony. Not pretty, but we were in business. The dream was in action! Now came the opportunity to mold the business how we wanted and implement our ideas.

We had decided to move close to the boatyard so that we could show boats and focus on our customers. At the same time, we started hosting events for the customers to get to know us because while there were people who didn't like the Darby's, others did, so we had to win all of them over.

We took a strong value driven approach to running the business. I had the benefit of seeing some of the great things that could be accomplished during my days at Abbott–the employee profit share, complete team buy-in on being part of the solution. We built KYS on the values we were raised with–family, integrity, employee experience, value to the customer, and a high-level customer experience.

We had to earn the customer's trust, and this was part of our business plan. We hosted a lot of get-togethers and began the tradition of having a pre-Chicago Boat Show get-together at the office. In the past, Joe and Elaine had just given tickets out to the boat show, no strings attached. We changed it to bring people in, so we got a chance to meet them, and then we gave out tickets.

We usually would host speakers and different seminars. We built a customer affinity process to build that relationship and trust. That went a long way with the older generation.

Jake and I were in our late thirties, so we attracted a lot of people like us—single income, no kids, double income, no kids, or double income, and maybe one or two kids that had just started.

We continued to mold the business and results started to take root. One of the ways this became evident was attracting boaters in our age range (mid-late thirties) this simple act drew the average age of our client down because like attracts like, and that was a positive outcome.

Here we were, two guys that had no background in running a Marine dealership but had a lot of great ideas and life experience. I think that's what our brand partner had bought into, and we really hit the ground running. The first year we decided we were going to pool a lot of our sales through Jake because the business couldn't support both two incomes, so I wasn't going to leave my job right away.

We inherited the sales team. That was one of the deals that I made with the Darby's, that we would bring over the one sales guy, Stan. We also brought over the service guys which was a big deal because service was everything, and critical to our core value of delivering a great customer experience.

I remember meeting with Jose, Renee, and Elizandro, and saying we weren't going through with the deal unless they came with. I told them we needed them, and it was going to be different. Not only did we tell them that, but we showed them. It was also a sense of pride for them to be working for a company owned by one of their own kind–a testament to the fact that representation matters.

ENJOYING SUCCESS

We had some smashing great success right out of the gates in 2002-2005. Every year we exceeded our goal. We won Top Gun not only for sales but also for customer service.

These were excellent years, selling tons of boats, so we started looking ahead to what was next. That turned out to be moving down the road to a couple of storefronts over on 2001 South Halsted, which was a bigger office, and we took on a guy from the dealership in Detroit that had closed.

We continued to do well in 2005-2007, and started thinking about how we could build more equity into the business. When we first started the business, we had to get a letter of credit, so that meant locking up $500,000 of capital to get a $1 million line of credit because we have two guys in business that didn't have the background, and the Darby's had no value in the business other than goodwill. So, it was a tough run, and that led to us being a bit cash strapped at the beginning.

Once we developed the floor plan, Transamerica, who was the lending company, then gave us a full line of credit. They released the letter of credit, as our sales and pipeline supported the projections we had made, and we got that money back as operating capital. We had been doing well and had a great year, so we decided to buy a building.

Where should we buy? Crowley's had now moved down

to the Southeast Side, our old neighborhood, just blocks from where we had grown up. We started looking all over the city for different locations. Did we want to be close to the North Side where a lot of the money is? But we couldn't find a location that worked for storefronts. They were either too expensive, they weren't conducive to our business, or they were just hard to get to.

BUILDING OUR DREAM

We finally found a location at 3635 South Halsted, and it was a gutted-out old laundromat. When we saw the building, it was for sale by the owner, and when I called the number, nobody answered. I looked in the window, and there was no flooring, and the floor supports had been ripped out and were gone.

Someone had started rehabbing the building and just stopped. I think they realized it was too much of a project. So, the owner figured he was just going to flip it as is. It seemed like a good opportunity, and we figured out what it would cost to rehab the building. We went and got a construction note to cover what we had planned. We did all of that. We closed on that property and started building our dream location.

Meanwhile, we moved into a vacant office next door for the time being, at 3637 South Halsted, so we could be close to the construction project. Being a total gut rehab, it took us about seven months to finalize the rehab. We opened the doors in January 2007, and then, of course, the recession hit.

HIT BY THE RECESSION

The fall of 2008, I remember being at the Annapolis boat show, which was our annual national show to attend. Our dealer meetings were run prior to the start of the show. We went to our dealer meetings, and then the foot traffic and buzz turned to the turmoil in the markets. Interest went to nothing. People were worried with Lehman Brothers having gone down that September and signaling a crumbling of the global economy. Everybody was on their phones, looking at what the heck was going on. Then the markets took a dive that next week, and we went into a full-on recession. That was a record year for low sales.

In our usual fashion, we asked ourselves, what next? My youngest daughter had just been born that August. We had just built the new office, and then in January 2009 my wife lost her job. She was working at a large financial institution, and they laid her off. I remember the day I got my call from Sonia, saying she had bad news.

She said they laid us off because they don't have enough to support everybody, and they are making a lot of changes with the recession and everything. This series of events marked the start of a very challenging time for our country and as a business owner with a family, probably some of the most difficult experiences I would have encountered to date.

Our first move was to pull the girls out of daycare and watch them at home. We had moved into our new Bridgeport house in 2006, and now we had this new building and business to support. We were making it work on whatever income we could get and were eating away at our life savings and everything else to try to get things to happen.

I think every day, we looked at it to see how we could persevere through it. There were a lot of very difficult times, and the one thing we committed to the employees at the business was that we would do everything we could to keep things afloat. Our team helped by being scrappy in every way they could. The stark reality of being a business owner kicked in–sometimes you pay your employees before you pay yourself. Often, we would get ourselves into that realm of forgoing our own needs in order to make payroll.

I ended up leaving J&J in 2005, following the acquisition of Alza, and had gone full-time into Karma Yacht Sales because we had every reason to believe it would be able to support us. We had just paid off the entire business in 2004, and it was profitable the first year we owned it.

Now we're trying to decide, do we walk away from our dream? Do we shut the doors? I mean, the easy thing in hindsight would've been to shut the doors and walk away. I would've preserved a lot of my equity in my own portfolio, but I said we're going to keep punching through this. I would say 2007-2010 were the difficult years, trying to make ends meet and trying to stitch deals together.

We would have open houses to try to introduce deals to our customers, but people weren't buying it. The one nice thing about the whole process was that the customers that had really bought into the community that we had built-- because now we were already seven years into our open houses—every year, they looked forward to that January open house.

People started saying, "You know what? I was about five years off from buying a new boat, so I'm going to buy my boat now if you can sell the one that I've got." We would work deals out to sell their boats and then roll them into a new one. That saved us because I can tell you, there were sometimes when, just as things seemed very dark, and we were going to have to close the doors, all of a sudden, we would get a phone call from a customer.

And that customer would say the same as all the others who had saved us before—we were a couple of years off, but we like you guys, and we're going to buy a boat. Can you put us in that boat? We're going to sell our boat. Can you sell it? We would manufacture a deal, and this is when you realize how people are, what people are made of. The customer experience paid back in dividends. Our mantra of good fortune follows admirable actions that come to life.

THE RESET

We limped along for a few years until about 2010, when we were blessed by acts of grace from many little angels who provided funding and more importantly purchased products. Through our South Side scrappiness, we nursed the business back to life. Then things started picking up a little bit, and we started seeing some sales. The big difference being that the American recreational boating market was not coming back to the pre-recession volume.

Our sales were down about 60, almost 70, percent. In trying to figure out how we would grow again, we took on a couple of different lines to try to expand the portfolio, lines that we could work with without having to take on additional debt.

These new lines weren't as popular in the states, and the designs were very appropriate for Europe but not for the American buyer. We dabbled in trying to expand our business and did a lot of service business to try to keep the doors open. Even with that, we had to continue to put cash in the business to keep it running, and then we reached a point where I think Jake was pretty tapped out, and he had borrowed from family and friends, and every avenue he could. Our ownership equity had become unbalanced.

I reached a point where I thought, if this doesn't turn quickly, I don't know how much more capital I want to dump into this. Then, things started turning around in 2010, and then 2011 was a little better. 2012 was a little better yet, and 2013 was better than 2012. We started coming back, but it was tough, and I would call the period from 2009 through 2013 the reset years because it was a massive adjustment to the business trajectory we were on prior to 2008. We had to reset everything because the new normal was not like the old normal. That's where we doubled down on a lot of stuff, and it was difficult.

A FRIENDSHIP FALTERS

The relationship with Jake had changed a lot during that period of time. We went from the guys in the early part of that decade that we're hanging out, sailing a lot, drinking beers, and playing hockey. And then life seemed to get in the way.

As would be expected, our families became our priority, the challenges of the struggling business also added complexity to our relationship. These were echoes of my dad's comments when I was younger about not doing business with friends and family because of the emotional component.

We started growing distant as opposed to hanging out as friends. Now it had become more about the business. When you work with somebody all day long, you really don't want to see them at night or on weekends. The reality of that started to kick in, and it was then, in early 2012, that I got involved a lot more with the Chicago Yacht Club.

CHAIRMAN OF THE RACE TO MACKINAC

I was on the Mac committee since 2004 and was tapped to be the chairman of the Mac committee in 2012 and 2013, on the back end of the wing nuts accident in 2011 when a boat capsized, and two people died. I was vice-chair during that year. My new role as chairman required more effort, and I still had a lot of responsibilities at Karma Yacht Sales, but my new position did give Karma Yacht Sales a lot of exposure.

One of the things that we got involved in heavily from the start of the business was becoming advocates for the product in the racing community. We bought our first race boat in 2003 and then, four years later, bought another one in 2007. We were campaigning the boat heavily and became very visible ambassadors for the brand. We had a lot of successes, and that helped the business. We won the Race to Mackinac in 2004, '05, '06, '08, '09, '11, '14 and '15.

That unprecedented success drove recognition and sales. Our racing program and the business became a fundamental pillar of the Lake Michigan racing community. Over a period of 15 years, we placed either first, second, or third, 13 out of those 15 years. It's quite a record on top of winning other regattas in different races. We became advocates for the product and built a strong community around that. We owned a 36.7, which was the boat that we had during the period that we owned and built that fleet. That model ran for about 10 years, and we sold 36 of those boats new.

Then we sold another seven resales when people traded in or sold older boats. So, throughout the course of having a dealership, we sold 41 of those boats, built the fleet on Lake Michigan to be one of the strongest fleets nationally–you could even say internationally. To this day, there are still 16 or 17 of those boats racing in Lake Michigan. We still have our boat, and it felt good to build something and be a part of founding something that has lived on past your time.

We also built the same thing in the 40.7 community. It was a larger version of our boat, and not as popular because it's a little more expensive—and more expensive to run— but they're a very passionate group of people that built support for the product on top of the many other cruisers that we sold. For every race boat that we sold, we sold four cruisers. So you can imagine the community that we've built over the years.

A COMPANY IN TRANSITION

As we were clawing our way back, our lead brand had gone through their own changes. They had transitioned out of their American leadership team into a French leadership team and restructured the entire organization. The new guy that they brought in, Jean, was quite the character.

The stereotype that French tend to be a little difficult to deal with at times may have factored into this transition, and Jean was the embodiment of that. The American dealer network had developed into a strong family–a supportive community, and the change that was afloat was tough to transition into.

Our key brand partner had transitioned from being a large privately-owned business into a larger corporation with a board of directors, and the granddaughter of the founder retained a seat on the board, but they had brought in investors and became a publicly-traded company. Big changes came that impacted many of us in the dealer network.

In working with our lead brand, we started to see them change from the company that we had originally started to do business with and liked when they approved us as a dealer. They were about their dealer network and helping them be successful because they realized that their success came when their dealers were successful.

Now, with this new leadership, they were very driven on deliverables and metrics that had to be hit, but the difficulty came with the personalities that were involved, and that's where Jean was a difficult individual.

He did and said different things, which breeds a lot of mistrust. They started listening less to their dealers and started doing more of what they wanted, which was very different from what we had experienced. We had always been, from the very early days, a part of their dealership council, which is involved in making the decisions around product, sales, marketing, and promotion, where we had a say and a seat at the table, helping guide the direction of the company in the US. Often what is good in Europe isn't always good in the United States.

Then there was the Jean factor, and a lot of the dealers had a great disdain and distrust for him. I think it corroded the strong and galvanized dealer leadership group that they had created over the many years that we had been a part of. Language barriers, lack of emotional intelligence, breaches of trust all factored into a cycle of conflict. What made it most difficult for us, is that we began this journey as customers–fans of the product, and in spite of the personality challenges, we still loved the product. To this day, I love the product. It became unbearable and financially taxing at a time when we were battle weary from having survived the recession.

END OF THE ROAD

So, 2014 rolls around, and we're going through a new transition. The reason behind it goes back to the time when we were in negotiations to buy the business, and Joe had lost the state of Michigan as part of his territory because he didn't want to open an office in Michigan. As a result, our lead brand put a dealership there that was primarily dedicated to a competing brand, in our opinion.

We tried to go back to Joe at the time and renegotiate the deal, but he wouldn't. That should've been a sign for us to walk away from it. The person I am today would've been a lot sterner with Joe and Elaine than I was at that point, and age gives you that perspective. But at the time, we were two young guys in our late thirties, and we wanted this dream. We were in love with this dream, and we wanted to see it come to fruition. You might say we violated rule number two of negotiation—always be willing to walk away.

We had lost that part of the territory, which was accountable for about two to three boats a year, in the grand scheme of things. We looked at it as water under a bridge. They told us that at some point in the future, we could probably try to get it back. And throughout the course of having the dealership, the dealers that they put in place there did very little to sell boats.

They stocked the minimum that they had to, yet when they came to the Chicago boat show, we had to always stock the boats, put the boats there, set them up, and staff the booth, which cost us between $30,000 to $40,000. We received co-op marketing subsidies for that, but it had always been a chafing point for us because the other dealer never carried their weight in that process, and we felt that they pulled the same amount of leads out as we did. If anything, they paid 10 percent of what we paid.

Every year it was a high overhead cost to pay for fewer leads, and then there was the wear and tear on the boats and labor to set it up, tear it down, and repackage the boats in the middle of the Chicago winter. We started telling our brand partner that we wanted the other dealer to pay their weight. This Jean guy agreed that in 2014 we were going to split it in half, but the other dealer said no.

We made a federal case out of it, so in 2015 they said we were the lead, and they would bill it evenly. We paid a little less in '15, but it still wasn't equitable. Then, as '16 rolled around, we started making a big issue out of it in the middle of the year, and this is when Jean started shoving all these requirements down our throats. We told them if you want to be represented at this show, which is the biggest show for their area, it must be equitable.

We met in late fall, and they seemed to agree, saying they just needed us to be the lead. And then he went silent on us. November comes and goes, and then it's December. We receive a 'Dear John' letter telling us that they were going to assign the Southeast Wisconsin part of our territory to the Michigan dealers. That floored us, as they told us to our faces that there would be no changes. Add to all of this, my dad's passing on December 20, 2015, and you have a turmoil with decisions that were staring us down.

I was trying to deal with losing my dad, and we had the show opening up at the beginning of January 2016. We still hadn't heard anything, so I fired off an email to him that we needed to get on a call the first of the year. We had the call on Jan. 6, and Jean and his national sales manager jump on the call.

We asked them what was going on with the show because they hadn't paid for anything, and nothing had been done. Their response was to tell us, you guys set it up, and we'll work it out on the back end. We said no because we trusted them in 2015 and we still got stuck paying for most of it. We went back and forth, and they're not budging. They want us to continue to work last year's deal out, and one more time, we tell them no way, Jose.

We're cash-strapped at this point because of decisions we made to try to grow the business. We anticipated this happening, and we had scripted this out before we jumped on a call. We heard them out, engaged in the discussion and eventually I said, effective at the end of this call, I'm sending a letter to France telling him that we're resigning as your representative. And if they want to know why we'll tell them it's because you don't have any integrity in how you do business.

Jean asked, how do we right-side this situation, and I told him if he had to ask that at this point in the game, he's already lost. He hadn't been listening to us, he had no integrity, and he was a snake. I ended by saying, "We're done with you," and hung up.

We sent the letter firing our key brand manufacturer and then wrote a carefully crafted letter to all our customers to let them know we would be transitioning, and that much to our disappointment we were no longer carrying the brand.

MOVING ON

Now, it's 2016. We just fired our manufacturer that made up close to 60 percent of our revenue. You can argue that it wasn't the smartest thing to do. We had just done what someone at my dad's wake had warned me of. They said, "Lou, don't make any hasty decisions about your life in the next two to three months because right now you're in a very fragile state."

That's ringing in the back of my head, and I couldn't help but wonder, did I totally screw it up? It didn't matter, though, because, at that point, there was only one path, and that was moving forward.

Now we had to tell our employees what happened. We explained the situation and said we didn't know yet what that meant for the future, but we would have to make some changes. In the meantime, we needed to finish the work we had in the house and would meet again the next week when we knew more.

That next meeting was really hard. We had gone through the financials and looked at how much cash we had, the revenue that was coming in, and in the end, had to tell them we were letting them go. It was a tough decision, and it was about to get even harder.

While I thought January 6, 2016 was the second toughest day of my life—as the day we ended our business relationship with our manufacturer. That would only be the first in a series of difficult challenges I would face.

Throughout this highly stressful period in our lives, I won't lie, it was difficult. The highs of business ownership were very high, the sense of fulfillment and accomplishment of bringing your dream into the world–manifesting it. It was a very special period in my life, a second to becoming a father in real life. The many lessons we learned, some by falling down, shaped my perspective and skills as a business owner and operator.

You might say this was a crash course (pun-intended) in business. The parallel personal challenges only heightened the challenges I faced. While I did not know it then, this experience would just increase my skill set as a business leader and test my faith like no other time in my life.

CHAPTER 14:

THE COMEBACK

"Do not judge me by my success, judge me by how many times I fell down and got back up again."

~ Nelson Mandela

The period between January 6, 2016, when we hung up the phone after firing our boat manufacturer, and Memorial Day was extremely volatile. It didn't seem that way at first, but all the signs were there—it was coming, and I didn't have to wait long.

After we hung up, me and my partner, Jake, sat there trying to make sense of all that had just happened and what that meant for the future—ours and Karma Yacht Sales.

Jake and I talked about it for a little while and confirmed that this was the path we'd chosen, so we hit send on the email that officially severed our ties with the boat manufacturer we had represented for many years.

I still had the warning a friend gave me ringing through my head—don't make any major life decisions for a few months following the passing of my dad. I think if I had to do it over, I might have done it differently. What I learned at the back end of that whole year and the next two years is that everything is negotiable. And I think a lot of things would've been highly negotiable.

Jake was a very risk-averse person, while I was more of a risk-taker. So, I think that in his head, he was struggling with his own personal financial situation, and thanks to firing our manufacturing partner, we had significant business debt and little projected income to leverage and pay it.

If I had that same moment to relive over, I would've negotiated my way out of it, but there was no turning back the clock. We both made the decision, so it was ours to ride through. The rest of that week was an emotional mess because normally, at that time of year, we would be prepping and getting ready for the show. It was like losing a limb because suddenly we didn't know what to do. We unwinded everything we had to do with the show, sent the letter to all of our customers, and explained our decision.

GREAT CUSTOMER RELATIONSHIPS MATTER

As it turned out, a handful of them were going to go buy boats that year at the show, and they held off on their purchases. They said, "We're not going to buy them until we find out what you're going to do. Then we'll buy the brand of boats that you represent." We had a good following and a very strong reputation for being fair business people in the marine industry.

I think there are very low expectations of marine professionals. One, because some of these guys do this for a labor of love or to finance their hobbies. They're either sailors or boaters, and this satisfies their desire to be on the water, so they go at it with a less than professional approach, and it's unfortunate because I think it sets the bar really low.

In my assessment of the market, when you say what you do and back it up with action, that sets you up for success. It was easy to build our market share up, so I thought maybe things had changed. The recession had changed the market, but I felt that we could still build ourselves back up with another brand.

We had sister brands courting us. We had competing brands that wanted us, too, so we had our pick. The thing that's funny about the marine industry is that regardless of the brands you represent, it's mostly about relationships at the end of the day, and this is something that marine manufacturers don't get sometimes. They think that because they build a brand, they make the boat, and the brand is the draw.

I find that it really takes both. It's part of the appeal because you need a good product to bring a customer in. But the last nine yards of that is on the dealer, and it's on that distribution channel. You can buy a boat from anyone, but it's buying that second and third boat where the relationship comes in. There's trust that's been built over time.

I brought myself back to our 10-year company anniversary, and I remember sitting there talking at the event that we held at the yacht club. As I was talking to different people in the room, thanking them for their business, customers would say, "You've done a phenomenal job in turning this brand around in Lake Michigan. What you've done with 36.7 on the race circuit is phenomenal, and it is enviable. What you've done with the brand in terms of customer service has been incredible."

It was true, and we had the awards to prove it. We were a perennial Top Gun award winner for sales and also for service, and we had acquired 100 percent CSI scores in multiple years, which was unheard of because somebody is always going to ding you for something, dropping you into the 90s.

ADVOCATING FOR OUR CUSTOMERS

For us, that was a testament that our formula worked, and I think that's where the marine manufacturers always underestimate the value of that relationship. Even now, as we talk about the digitization of customer relationships, the Amazon approach, selling stuff direct, virtual, or digital, there's still a need to touch and feel. It's a significant purchase, and there's a need to develop a relationship with that and assure them of what they're getting. Boats are like houses--something's going to go wrong with them, no doubt about it—and you're going to need the dealer to be your advocate.

That's what manufacturers don't understand--that we become the ally for the customer. We become the advocate because when they push back on the customer regarding the warranty, reimbursements, and the like, sometimes we will eat that, and we did over the course of our 15 years in business.

The mantra that we built the business on is customer service and doing for others what we would like to have done for ourselves. I think that's where the marine manufacturers missed the boat; no pun intended. The strength of the bond that developed between the customer and the dealer transcends everything else. As we talked to more and more customers, they kept saying, "We liked the brand, but we loved you and the service you provided!

As dealers, we started to see the impact of product decisions on our market share. These were all the factors that led up to that January 6 decision—the market changes, the pricing changes, the leadership changes, and it started to become a very challenging situation.

THE GENERATION GAP

At that time, I was involved in various committees in the marine industry, and we started to see that sailing wasn't coming back from the recession at the rate that it needed to. There were people that were in the sport who were older, and the Marine industry hadn't done a good job of reaching out to younger boaters.

We all knew the demographics of baby boomers and where they were eventually going. There weren't enough Gen Xers to fill the gap, and Millennials were completely disengaged from it because they were broke, had challenges paying student debt back, and were probably not planning to buy a boat.

So, there's that whole disconnect between the end consumer and the marine industry combined with product improvements and product changes that were not being well received by the market. Not really listening to customer insight, as our manufacturing partner didn't want to hear what the American market wanted. In addition, we had made various attempts to bring in revenue. We were looking at service, and we were doing management of people's boats to bring in money.

BANKRUPTCY IS NOT AN OPTION

At this time, Jake was in a very fragile state from a financial perspective. He was up to his chin in personal debt. As a business, we had a significant amount as well. He had started to present the idea of filing bankruptcy as soon as we came back from the Christmas holiday in 2015. I think he couched it first as a way forward, a plan B if we couldn't get a second brand.

While it might have been an option, it wasn't a path that I was comfortable taking. I had a wife in financial services, and I was on the board of a bank, so going into bankruptcy was not going to bode well with me. It would significantly impact my wife and my standing in the financial services industry also.

Jake was trying to present it as a way for us to jump together into the pool because we were 50/50 operating partners. As I continued to say no, that wasn't what I wanted to do, Jake became a lot more anxious, and we still had no stable foreseeable revenue strain.

I could understand his source of concern and anxiety. I had the same worries, too, and it's not like I was sitting on a ton of cash because I was going to be eating through what I had put away pretty quickly.

I'd take it a different path, though. Since leaving the pharmaceutical industry in 2005, I had a few side ventures and investments that I kept active and provided some residual income for me. It had allowed me to save some money to invest and to put in different areas where I had money to sit back on.

Going back to our original operating agreement, we were 50/50 partners, but recession unleveled that arrangement because when we put money into the business to keep it afloat, I had more to put in and more resources at my disposal. So, to keep things alive, I put in more than my fair share.

When we started the business, we started with a level arrangement, we were friends, and there was a lot of goodwill in starting out as 50/50 partners.

There were big lessons for me, too, on equity and balance during a partnership. I go back to the lessons my dad taught me, and one of them was don't do business with family and friends because when they go wrong, they go really wrong.

I was starting to see as time went on that this wasn't going to go well, and it probably wasn't going to end well, either. I remember a lot of times when I was alone getting pretty emotional about it. I wished I could reach out to my dad and ask, "Hey, dad, what would you do in this situation? How would you unwind this to be able to preserve the relationship?"

LONGING FOR MY DAD'S WISDOM

I don't know if there was a good way to unwind it. My dad, during his youth, had to make some very difficult decisions. It took me back to one specific incident I remember as a child. My dad had a brother who had a substance abuse problem, and he might have been bipolar. I never knew for sure. He never shared with me what the real reason was, but we would go to church on Sunday, and this brother, the one closest in age to him as my dad was the youngest child, would always be waiting for him in the parking lot.

He knew to wait for my dad there because he knew we went to church every Sunday, and he knew which mass we went to. He would hang out there, and he would approach my dad, all disheveled and smelling like a homeless guy. I was never afraid of him, and I remember on a couple of occasions, dad would bring him to our house. He would ride in the backseat with us, and when we got home, he would take a bath, dad would give him a fresh set of clothes, and feed him a warm meal.

Then he'd take him back to the halfway house where he lived, and he'd give him some money. I think it was difficult for my dad because he felt that in giving him the money, he was enabling his destruction. I remember eventually going to my uncle's funeral because he did succumb to alcoholism, or it led to his demise. It was a really difficult thing for my dad, and I think my dad tried doing everything he could.

So, I would go back to the conversations about that with my dad when I would ask, "What would you have done differently with Uncle Jose? What would have saved him?" And my dad would say, "I don't know that there is a way to change things when someone or something is on a path to end. It just is, and you've got to understand that it's out of your hands. You could pray a lot for it, but it's going to end up the way it's going to end up. There's nothing you can do to change it."

OUR PARTNERSHIP STARTED FALLING APART

I could see the similarities to what I was going through with Jake and the business. There were decisions we made in the business, decisions that Jake made personally, and decisions that I made personally that got us to that point. Some of them were good decisions, and some of them weren't. I think we could have sat there, and we could have blamed each other for them, but we made the best decisions we could with the information we had at the time.

And I think Jake, if he was to be fully honest with himself, would say that he made the best decisions he could at the time to keep his family going and he knew that for me, it was really difficult.

There were decisions we made that became glaring reminders of things we should have cleaned up a long time ago—the inequities in the relationship and the inequities in the business partnership. In the back of my mind is my dad saying don't do business with family and friends, but it's too late to say that now because I made that choice.

For the most part, our business and our relationship as friends and business partners went smoothly. We had a lot of good times, and we were good friends. I felt bad for his situation. There were a lot of things he did at the end that made it even more difficult.

You know, everything's a matter of perspective, and I'm sure it was tough for Jake to be put in the position of having to decide between work that was bringing money into the house, probably less so at that point, and friendships and his relationship, his marriage, with his wife and keeping the peace there. And let's not be dummies; we knew where that was going to go. I mean, he'd be stupid not to side with his household.

A FRIENDSHIP AT RISK

The whole situation corroded our friendship. I could see that he was in dire financial straits and needed cash. When it came to the boat we owned and operated together, he committed to us that he was going to find a way to work it out. We told him we were happy to let him out, and we would continue to pay for his part of the operating costs of the boat. We told him he could still sail with us, we're still friends, he said he would but eventually reneged. Jake was a little closer to some of our crew members than Marty and I were, and I put that down to our cultural differences.

For Marty and I, our families were everything, and we had a large extended family. So, given our preferences, we would spend time with each other and our families, because that's our world, whereas, with a lot of our crew, the boat became their family. While we were all friends with everybody that was on our crew, I think the divide between Jake and me and the business became difficult for some of them.

One of our crew members was getting married in Pittsburgh, but Marty, and I made the decision that we needed to save money and not go. It wasn't the time for us to be attending a lot of things.

So, we tightened things up a little bit because we had to put our boat in the water and run the syndicate. We were preparing for the 25th passage for one of our crew members--it was their goat year, and that was going to require a little bit of capital. So, we didn't go to that wedding, but Jake and a few of our crew members did.

THE PARTNERSHIP ENDS

Jake decided to cut ties and walk away from our business. The turmoil of this period in time was excruciatingly difficult, and Jake's decision triggered a series of other factors that had to be handled. It led to a state of distress

Now, I had to figure out how this was going to work, so I went back to our operating agreement.

I read it a few times, read it a few times more, and it said if one person decides to leave the partnership, the other partner has a right to continue the business as a sole proprietor. So, if Jake chose to walk away, he walked away with nothing, unless he wanted his half of the debt. He said no, he wasn't going to do that, and I ended up having to close him out.

It was a very difficult decision because you're saying goodbye to a friendship, too. Could it have been preventable? Could it have been handled differently? I don't know. Like much of life, you handle as best you can with what information you have at your disposal. You protect your self-interests and those of your family. In the end, it was what Jake was doing also.

SAILING TOGETHER ONE LAST TIME

We agreed that we were going to allow him to continue to sail with us. We said, let's sail this, we've got this thing to do for Christina, our crewmate that was doing her 25th. Let's do it and not let all of this stuff ruin it. So, we did that, and then the crew fell apart.

I think sailing together was a painful reminder. We did okay that year and finished third in the race. It wasn't our best performance. We wanted to finish in first for Christina's sake, but there were a lot of things at play leading into that, and there was a very toxic influence that we had from one of our former tacticians that we had kicked off the crew the previous year.

ENCOURAGEMENT, FRIENDSHIP, AND A YIDDISH PROVERB

After Jake walked out of the business, I had to right side the business and help nurse it back to life. I went back to what I learned from the recession—to start from the baseline again, strip out all the costs, and get down to what's necessary and build revenue streams incrementally.

One of our mutual and good friends, Warren Levins, was also a customer of ours and about my dad's age. He had bought his boat from us and had been a big fan and supporter of our business.

We competed against him in the 36.7 fleet, and he was a remarkable gentleman, very generous, and we had developed a friendship over time. He was almost like a father to me and called the office one day while I was trying to find my sanity during the chaos with Jake. He said, "Let's get together for lunch."

We met and talked for a long time. Warren had an interesting relationship with his business partner, who he owned a textile company with. At some point, Warren had gotten himself into some challenging times with his company. His business partner was tough about it and said he was out. That split the relationship, and Warren then went to another friend of his who bought the company from Warren. What was left of it, Warren kept himself as sole proprietor, and the friend who had bought the company kept Warren on as president. The new owner was graceful and remained the sole investor in the business.

This man saved Warren and also allowed him to continue in his specialty trade. As Warren and I talked about that experience, one of the things he remembered was how he would talk to his mom a lot. She shared an old Yiddish proverb with him where the women in a complex would hang laundry outside and help each other, sometimes bringing in others' laundry if they were busy, there was congeniality to a limit, but the moral of it said, "When it rains, everyone cuts for their own laundry."

He looked at me and said, "Lou, with all you have here, you have to do what's best for your family. It's all about saving your ass. That's all that Jake's doing. I wouldn't take it as personal, and you wouldn't expect him to do otherwise. It's just what it is; it's human nature."

The highlight of that was it's all about self-interest at the end of the day, and people are going to do what's best for them. Warren added, "And that's what you've got to do. You had a good run in this business. You can get out of it, and I know you can figure out what's next. You're a very resilient guy. You're smart. You get people, and you get businesses. You just have to figure out what the next thing is for you."

FLASHBACKS TO DAD'S STRUGGLE

Life would be so much easier if we could compartmentalize the personal issues and address things as they come along. In a perfect world, that would be wonderful. That is not what the world is about. For me, the period from 2012 through 2016 was filled with many personal issues to balance, mostly related to my father's health. My father's later years of life were filled with treatments for his chronic asthma and breathing issues. He was paying the price for all the years of working in a steel mill with lax OSHA regulations and chronic exposure to many airborne contaminants–a common affliction of retired steelworkers.

While no epidemiologic study has ever been done of the area in which I grew up in, the steady listing of neighbors and friends who have come down with cancer is more than a coincidence. Leaching of heavy metal contaminants into the water source or airborne pollution are logical culprits; however, the definitive connection has never been made.

Dad had suffered from chronic obstructive pulmonary disease (COPD) for quite some time. He was on a formulary of medications to control his airway issues. I lost track of the number of calls and visits to the hospital with him requiring rescue steroid therapy and medical intervention. His treatments with the anticoagulant coumadin made it difficult to run routine blood tests for other issues he might encounter. I often thought that this was an unfair sentence for a man that had done so much for me. I would have gladly switched places with him just so he could have some normalcy.

In 2012 Dad was diagnosed with advanced stage IV prostate cancer. I remember meeting with him and his internal medicine doctor and urologist to ask the difficult questions—such as "What next?" They would tell us that needing to be on the coumadin made it hard to run regular blood tests and catch the cancer sooner. It also limited treatment options. If it wasn't so advanced, I would have made a federal case out of that, but we decided to push ahead. His doctor and I decided that high dose hormone associated therapy and sex hormone suppression (i.e., Leuprolide acetate injections combined with bicalutamide) was the preferred route.

Dad did not want to undergo seed therapy or chemo (and he couldn't), so we began the journey of ups and downs. The doctor would not commit on what to expect or worse yet- life expectancy because each case is different. With God's divine grace and much patience and prayers–for over a period of three years, dad evaded the undertaker. It was challenging because his favorite summer trip was to Mackinac Island to see his boys sail in, and during that time he was too weak to make the trip.

Finally, in the Summer of 2015 he was able to make the trip—riding scooter and all—but he had a grand time. It wasn't until his check-up on October 19, 2015, that we got the news that the cancer had metastasized into every one of dad's major organs and our options were fatally limited. I asked his doctor to be straight with me on the predicted outcomes to which she replied, "Lou, if you would have told me that your dad would be alive today three years ago,

I would not have believed it, but here he is, your dad is a fighter. I don't know if it is thirty, sixty, or ninety days–it is up to him." After the visit, I remember asking dad what he wanted to do. If he wanted to keep fighting. Did he still have it in him? To which he replied, "No Louie, I'm tired–no more."

Dad would leave us the morning of December 20, 2015, sixty-one days after meeting with his doctor. I was blessed that I had one last night with him on the 19th. Sonia, the girls and I visited with him and mom. Dad sat in his usual chair supervising the decorating. He was rather pensive that night. I asked him what he was thinking and then dove into telling him about all the challenges I was facing.

Dad was listening, but clearly had his mind on other things. Until suddenly he stopped and said, "Louie, it's going to be ok. It always is." Those were my last words with dad. My man of steel would leave us the next morning.

BUILDING MY CONFIDENCE

I did a lot of soul searching in the period after 2016, and in 2017 I went to the Sailing Leadership Forum in San Diego. I had gotten to know a very generous gentleman by the name of Terry Kohler and his family. He was the son of the founder of the Kohler company.

Terry had a racing program for a long time. He flew us to the Forum in his private jet and was also part owner in Edgewater Boat Company, which owned North Sails for some time. On this trip from Sheboygan, Wisconsin, to

San Diego, California, we stopped in Nevada with Terry's daughter and toured their plant to see how the sails were made before continuing to the Forum.

I stayed with Lindy and Barb Thomas while in San Diego. Lindy was another gentleman that I knew from the club. We had served on the Mac Committee for a stretch of time. I had always looked up to him because Lindy was a self-made businessman with practical sense. On top of that he was a colorful and genuine person. He had also founded a boat company, Thomas Marine, Inc., and introduced his boat, the T-35.

He was a phenomenal businessman and had retired and, together with his wife, became Chicago snowbirds. They lived in Glenview, Illinois, a Chicago suburb, part of the time and in San Diego the rest of the time. Lindy was also a member of the San Diego Yacht Club.

That whole weekend, private jet and all, was a neat experience. Sort of what I needed to clear my head. I met a lot of great people at the Forum and had a chance to spend some time talking with Lindy. I told him I was at this crossroads and asked him what I should do. He said, "Listen, kid, don't worry about it. You're going to be fine. When you come up with your next great idea, you call me up, and I'll be the first to invest. I'm not worried about it. If you're involved in it, it's going to happen."

He gave me a big vote of confidence at a time when I needed it the most because I doubted my own ability to come out of this. After that, I sold off our buildings and began the scale down of the business.

It was then that I felt like I was walking alongside my grandfather, Antonio Diaz. He was a proud, resilient gentleman. He made candies, he worked at a boarding school, and he was a tailor. I was walking a similar path, doing whatever I could to supplement our income, and sometimes little angels would appear and give us new opportunities to hold us over. My grandfather used to say, "As long as you're not afraid to work hard, you'll never go hungry," and he was right.

As it would happen, I was also the Rear Commodore at the Chicago Yacht Club during that time. There I am, going through one of the toughest financial times of my life and at the same time having to lead a club of privilege. I thought, wow, this is a tale of two worlds.

When I look back on that stretch of road, what I remember the most was the willingness of people who knew me and their desire to lift me up. To inspire me and help me see that no matter how many times I fell, I could pick myself up again. The whole time, the words my dad shared with me on his last night with us- "It's going to be ok" resonated in my mind. And Dad was right- it was. I would pick myself up.

CHAPTER 15:

CALL TO THE WATER

---

*"A ship is safe in the harbor, but that's not what ships are made for." ~ **John A. Shedd***

When you look at lessons learned from the water, it's about taking risks, learning new things, and exploring new horizons. Water in its most simple element is a therapeutic, life-giving substance. Being on the water is very natural for me, and I feel comfortable there, which makes sense because 60 percent of our bodies are water, and I'm a Pisces.

Aside from that, being on the water presents the opportunity for adventure—a call to the days of the explorers of the 18th century who would visit distant lands. My visits, while more local in nature, hold the same mystique and serve the purpose of providing a departure, albeit temporary from the everyday.

I remember the day I learned to sail as vividly as if it had been yesterday. It was my first day at Boy Scout camp, and I had gone with the Morales family, leaving the South Side of Chicago, and driving five hours to Muskegon, Michigan.

They had three boys in scouting, and we had become friends through the troop, which made carpooling with them fun. We stopped in Holland, Michigan, for lunch at the Dutch Village, and when we got to camp, we were very excited.

The check-in process included bringing your stuff to your campsite and setting your tent up with your bunkmate, which had already been discussed at previous meetings. That year we were staying at the Wolverine North camp, which was one of my favorites because it was close to the marshy end of Lake Wolverine, and there were always a ton of frogs.

Our campsite was a short walk to the frog bridge, right on the lake's edge. There were some massive bowl rocks over there, and we would watch bullfrogs that were as big as a frying pan. When you stretched them out with the legs, they were a few feet long.

I am the kid that used to go to ponds and bring back tadpoles, frogs, and different things that I'd collect. So, I was in heaven at that campsite. After check-in and taking care of the tent at our campsite, it was time to go down to the main commissary, the main camp area, which is around the pool, and we had to do our swim out, where you had to tread water and swim the length of the pool a certain number of times.

After that, they gave us a circle tag with one of two colors that designated whether you could swim in the deep end or the shallow end, and that tag had to go with you. I was proud that year because I passed the full certification and signed myself up for the mile swim, which was swimming the length of Lake Wolverine. I think I was 14 if I remember correctly. You swam it with someone in a rowboat next to you, and you usually did it in the afternoon.

FALLING IN LOVE WITH SAILING

That summer was exciting. We had already planned a lot of the merit badges that we would work on at camp. I had all my different merit badges picked out, but I had one slot left, and I remember they asked what I wanted to choose for that last merit batch. I knew they had Blue Lake, where they did the sailing instruction with each of us on a Sunfish– simple colorful lightweight sailboats that were more of a small skiff.

Being an adventurous kid, I always liked to try new things, so I chose sailing, and I could hardly wait the two or three days until it was my turn. I remember taking the hike to Blue Lake so that I could start the training. I showed up early that day, and it began with an orientation and learning the safety gear and parts of the boat.

They checked out our swimming skills again, and you had to bring your tag with you. Having the advanced swimmer tag came with a lot of perks, and one of them was being allowed to earn the sailing merit badge. I had to go through the processes of learning the parts of the boat and being able to explain the safety part of it. Then, they took us out on the lake to teach us how to use the boat.

It was such a cool experience—I had never been on a boat like that. There was a moderate amount of wind because it was in the morning. Usually, you get a breeze in the morning, and then it dies down, and everything becomes becalmed during the middle of the day. Then, in the late afternoon, you will get some breeze again. So, it was kind of uneventful, but it was safe to practice capsizing the boat a couple of times along with the rest of the training.

I got comfortable on the boat, and I loved getting wet and jumping in the water, so that was a blast. The second day of class was when we had to profess what we were doing. It was a three-day class, and now we had to teach what we learned on day one to somebody else in the class and then, again, to somebody else. It was like a chain test. In doing so, it ingrained the material we learned.

The second day was a little windier, and the boat only had one sail. That made it easy because you either let it out or brought it in, went into the wind, or went downwind easing the sail to make it go fast. I got a chance to learn the different parts of the boat and how they contributed to the boat's speed, and, for me, it was cool to be able to go a little faster on the water and have control of it.

On day three, they gave us a chance to play on the boats, and that's when I got comfortable with it. It was basic instruction, and I wouldn't call myself a professional at that level, but it was an excellent introduction. I fell in love with it because, in my neighborhood, we didn't have that stuff. I grew up less than a mile from the lakefront, I would always skip rocks or walk the beach, but I never sailed on it. For me, this was a whole different world.

I went back to summer camp for the next few years afterward, and I would always make it a point to go to the sailing center and take out a boat to go sailing. I learned to love it, but then I went to high school, started playing other sports, and got away from it because I didn't have access to it.

I got away from the sport during most of high school and college. I remember once in college, we went on a retreat to Lake Geneva, and I got a chance to get on a boat then, which was a lot of fun, but I never did much sailing after that.

A FUN WAY TO MEET PEOPLE

Once I got into the workforce, my first job was with Abbott Laboratories. Some of the guys that worked in an adjacent department would sail J24s out of Waukegan Harbor. We talked over lunch one day, and they mentioned that they were always looking for crew.

They asked if I would be interested in going, and I said, sure, I'd love to go.

I didn't know the J24 that well, but they gave me a diagram of the boat that showed its anatomy and what all the lines did, and then they said not to worry, they would show me everything. I went, and being the new guy, they stuck me on the bow, so I was in charge of the front of the boat and the spinnaker pole. From there, I started going out on Thursday nights and racing with them—at first just for casual stuff and then more competitively.

It got to be a lot of fun, and I got into the competitive part. Then, my career took me from Chicago out to Seattle. That's where I started the side business. First, though, I started sailing at Seattle Corinthian in J24s on Lake Union. That was a blind move, a way to make friends while sailing in a city where I had no connections and didn't know anyone. Later, it helped me to start the side business and meet more people, which led to all the other races that I did.

My next work move allowed me to pick the next city, and I chose Miami, where I did more of the same, sailing the Havana Cup and Newport Bermuda Race. I got involved in the Southern Ocean racing circuit, the SORC, and was racing on larger boats as crew again, and mostly stuck on the bow again because being the newer guy, that's what I knew how to do.

The bow is a very active part of the boat, and you're always getting wet. It's usually where you put the newbies and the younger guys who are more agile. Now, in my later years, I try not to do the bow because you're going to end up with bumps and bruises and maybe even fall off the boat. The natural evolution is to work your way to the back of the boat.

JOINING THE CHICAGO YACHT CLUB

Then I moved back home in 1997, and we bought into the 1978 AMF Paceship that we named Chiquita. I owned that together with my brother, Jake, and another friend. It was a fun boat that we sailed a lot, casually, and did some PHRF racing. We would rent space on the Monroe Harbor sea wall for parties because we docked on a mooring ball. So, we would pull the boat up, invite our friends, and have parties.

That sea wall was adjacent to the Chicago Yacht Club (CYC). We would always see this lovely yacht club with docks that always held regattas, parties, and the Mackinac race sendoff party we would go to occasionally. I always told myself I'd love to do the Mac race some year. I remember how I came upon the CYC, and I wondered what it would take to join that club. So, one day when we had the boat docked, I walked around, through the guard gate, and over to the front desk where I asked how to join the club.

I asked if I needed to know somebody for sponsorship or something similar. The desk attendant said no, and the membership director introduced me to a few of their members—Bonnie Barski and her husband, Pete Styles and his wife, and a gentleman named Greg Freeman. They ended up endorsing and sponsoring me for club membership, and they didn't know me from Adam. We sat down for lunch, and I told them a little bit about my love of sailing and how I had this ugly little yellow sailboat called Chiquita.

I jumped head first into life at the club. I got into the community and was involved in the culture there. I started doing some regattas on different boats, and I wanted to participate in the Mac race. I joined the club in 1999 and quickly got bold a week before the Mac race—I put my name on a crew board and said I'd love to do the race if anybody has an opening at the last minute.

MY FIRST MAC RACE

In typical fashion, the Thursday before the race, which begins on Saturday, I got a call from Tom. He and Brian were co-owners of a Frers 33 named Mystified. One of their crew members couldn't make the trip, and they needed another person to do the bow, the least desirable position. They said, we'd love it if you can make it--this is what your job would be, and you need the following equipment. I told them I had all the equipment, and I was happy to do it. I was excited to do my first Mac race.

I think my responsibility was to bring Gatorade and my gear, of course. It was an amazing experience. We started in a fairly decent breeze, making our way North, and as the sun went down that night, the wind picked up. Two hours into the boat race, we had a good breeze of 12 to 13 knots, a little bit northeasterly.

The boat was heeling, and I remember going downstairs to use the head (restroom). There are two ways you can use the bathroom. You can go off the back rail or go down below, but since it was a little wet and bumpy, they said it's probably better that you go down below. So, I went down below, and they had one of these heads in the boat that was on the port side of the boat, and the boat was leaning to the port side.

Of course, as you're at the toilet, you're facing downwards at an angle. I undid my gear, and I'm trying to balance myself. I'm doing my business, and the boat catches a wave. I heard the call from above, and of course, the boat goes up and then comes down, really hard.

In coming down, my knee bumped into the head pump, which you use to flush the bowl. I fell into it, and I cracked the pump with my knee. The pump started spilling all this blue liquid all over the floor, and my heart sank because I broke the boat three hours into the race. I stuck my head out into the companionway and asked if anyone had some duct tape.

They asked why, and I told them. Brian came down, looked at it, and said, yeah, it's broken. The good news is we have a backup, but the bad news is that head's done for the race. So, the guys are going to have to go off the back of the rail from this point on, and the girls will have to use a bucket that fits perfectly inside the head, and when done, will have to take the bucket with your business in it and dispose of it.

I knew that the two ladies on the boat were not happy with the new guy, and it would likely be a source of discontent for the next two and a half days.

I was the only rookie on the boat, and there was a tradition that when you get to the island, the rookies have to jump into the water. It all plays off the fact that you smell and haven't bathed for three days. The water was ice cold but pleasant after being on a stinky boat for a couple of days.

Little did we know that when we arrived at the island, they had a generator go out, and there was no power on the island at all. The ice cream shops were giving away ice cream because it was all going bad, and they were giving away food because it was going to rot or trying to sell it for a discount so they wouldn't lose money on the inventory.

I stayed on the boat because I was the new guy, but the owner had a hotel room, and it was great, but we still had to take a cold shower because they had no way to heat the water. So, it didn't make it much more pleasant.

ROOKIES LEARNING LESSONS

It was an interesting first experience, but I was hooked. I loved it. The plan all along had been that I was going to do the race, and then I was going to come back and show my crew how to do it.

I'd done a lot of offshore races at that point, but this was the first time that I had navigated the race. I did a lot of listening and a lot of watching the navigator on SV Mystified so that I could learn it. In hindsight, deciding to race our boat as a team the next year was probably the stupidest thing we did. But it was an adventure nevertheless.

In 2000 we had bought a new boat, Karma, the 33.7 boat that we outfitted for the Mac, and I did all the provisioning.

We hadn't yet bought the business, and this first race was a crew of seven newbies and then there was me. Seven guys that had never done the race before. A bunch of friends that we cobbled together who had a love for the sport. Some of them had varying degrees of racing experience, and I remember, as we made our way up the lake, it was a lot of fun, and we were still learning the boat.

We had all the safety gear and everything else that we should have. I was in charge because I had the most experience on the water with distance races. That year, the race was hit by some pretty good winds from behind, so we were sailing in some amazing breeze going up the Michigan coastline. The first night we decided to make our crossover and navigate in because we thought the breeze would be closer to the shore, and this is what the newbies do—get suckered into going really close into the Michigan shore.

The breeze was coming off the shore, and we could smell the campfires and pine trees. That's how close we were, and that wasn't a good idea because the next morning, when the sun came up, the breeze went away, and we were stuck over there. It added a few hours to our time, but we had made all the mistakes that newbies typically make, and, eventually, the breeze ended up filling in from behind.

I think we saw 18-20 knots, and while the team had practiced on the boat, we weren't experts at the execution of the vessel. At one point, they had let the sheets out, and the spinnaker was cleated on one side and cheated in. The boat was on its side because we had allowed the spinnaker to fill in and dragged the boat, bringing the boat completely to its side. A full-on broach!

One of the guys on the boat, Kevin, was going to take it upon himself to fix it. He thought he knew a lot about sailing, and he was a decent sailor, but he said, I've got a knife, I'll cut the halyard. I told him no, we're not cutting the halyard; those cost $400. Plus, it's our only halyard, so if we cut that, we're done.

So, I put the climbing harness on and was going to work my way up the mast. They would raise me to the top, and I would release the shackle and bring the halyard back down. It worked, and the boat righted itself. We made a lot of rookie mistakes, a lot of things that we wouldn't do again.

It was a great first race that we talked about for years afterward and had lots of good stories. That's what you'd expect when you put seven rookies and one person that has done one race on a boat together. I think we ended up in the bottom third of the fleet overall, but we survived. I had the pride of being the only guy that stood on the boat when seven rookies decided to jump in the water when we got to the island.

THE KARMA II

In 2002, we purchased our next boat, the Karma II, which was a First 36.7 model. That year, we had just finished purchasing the dealership. We had built a hodgepodge crew of a bunch of different people from the Who's Who of sailing—a bunch of fun people that had sailed on different boats. We started doing Wednesday night races to get the team trained on the boat.

We raced in 2002 and 2003, and neither time had great results. Then, in 2004 we decided we wanted to go out and win it. One of the guys at the sail loft, where we had bought our sails, said, all right, I'll do the race with you guys. His name was Sam Moyle, and he was definitely an acquired taste, but he taught us all how to push the boat—how to push the 24-hour sailing strategy, maximize the route, and get the maximum performance out of the boat.

Our mantra was, "We have plenty of time to rest on the island; let's push it right now." He got the best performance out of us as a team. It just had its consequences because he was unpleasant to be with. You wanted to punch him sometimes.

I remember that first race we did; Sam was coming unhinged. He felt the need to stay up throughout the night because I don't think he had confidence in us that we knew what we were doing.

At one point, we were all conspiring—he's either going to go to sleep, or we're going to knock him unconscious and drag him down below because he was just getting to be unbearable. We finally got him to go to sleep, and we were leading the race at this point, and our closest competitors were about 10 boat lengths behind us.

At this point, we were in front, so we thought we were winning the race, but there are different points where you converge with the other fleet, and you could end up in a drag race again. You could be leading two-thirds of the race, get to that point, and then lose the entire race because you come up on somebody that got better breeze.

GRIZZLY TO THE RESCUE

As I'm looking in the long eyes (Binoculars), I look back, and I see that boat named Grizzly, she was our sistership, and suddenly, I see this young lady do a dive off the side of the boat, into the water. I rushed up and got on the radio saying, "Grizzly, is all your crew, okay?" And you can hear them. They said they had a person in the water but were already in the process of recovering her and bringing her back on board.

We found out later that somebody had skipped taking her medications. She'd gotten delusional and decided to jump in the water. They pulled her back on and continued their race, but we were ready to render assistance. The rules protect you against that kind of situation, and it's not like you'd lose anything. You'd render assistance and then ask for a redress later.

That lead worked out for us into the straits. The Mac race is built-in six legs. The first leg is from Chicago to the dunes. The next leg is to point Betsie, which is the entryway into the Manitou passage. The third leg is in the Manitou Passage. There's usually a race into Gray's reef and around can three, and then there's another drag race in the straits. We call them "races" because these are the different legs of the Mac where you might lose the race. The final race is from the bridge to the finish line.

At this point, we're getting in, and it is already Tuesday morning. It's a slow race for us at this point, and once you get past the bridge, you have to contend with the ferry traffic, and they create a wake that will always slow you down. We were running in on a very thin line for our spinnaker because the breeze was fairly light.

We were trying to keep our VMG, (velocity made good), and not kill the boat speed for the vessel. And we were up against another boat by the name of Padawan, who made their way up on us. You might have the lead, but all of a sudden, another boat could have a better breeze. We ended up getting into a gybing duel with them in the last mile.

So, we kept switching our sails and gybing with them all the way to the finish line. It was so close that we ended up crossing the finish line, 60 seconds in front of Padawan to win the race. That was our very first Mac race that we won, and we did it by 60 seconds. Wow! I think to this day, Chris Lamb, the owner of Padawan, will say that yeah, that's a day that lives in infamy for him.

We missed the awards, so they had a special award ceremony for us in the tent on Windemere point, and we got a chance to take a picture with our flag, smoke a few cigars, and celebrate our win. We were dead tired, but we had won our very first Mac race. We didn't expect it. In 2005 we had our second Mac race win, and then in 2006 was the first year that we sailed with Christina Cordero. She was one of the better lady racers—an excellent Helms woman—who was a great contribution to the team.

CRUNCH TIME

With Cristina on the team, and our second win in 2006, it was the year of our three-peat. It was the first year that we had three wins in a row. 2007 was an amazing year because it was the first year that we brought the new Karma, which was hull number 236, the current boat that we have to this day.

So, we're off to a great start, and we're going for a four-peat. We had a good start and first two days, and we have now led the fleet all the way up the lake into the straits. We're in a drag race in the straits, and we get ahead of all our competition. Now we're leading by probably 20 minutes, and then all of a sudden, I go down below to do something, and the call is made to go to the left of the bridge and come in hard on the wind so that we could go into the right side of the finish line and make sure that nobody snuck in on us from the south end of the straits which is where the wind was coming from.

Well, we went so far to the left of the center span that we ended up running aground on the bridge base from the old Mac bridge that used to be next to the new bridge. It's a flat piece of concrete that we hit while I'm down below, and I hear the boat just come to a crunch and a grinding stop. Christina's at the helm, and this is her third race with us. I look up, and her eyes are huge.

We dumped the halyard, we released the spinnaker, we got the main, and we got everybody to one side to see if we could heal the boat. We had a 20-minute lead, so time was of the essence. If we get outside help, or if we turn on our engine, we're disqualified. Everybody got to one side, and nothing happened. Next, we put somebody up on top of the mass so that their weight could serve as a fulcrum and bring the boat on a pivot so that we could try to float in off of there, but that didn't work either.

Next, we took the anchor and hoisted it off the top of the mast to see if we could anchor our way sideways to loosen the keel and get off that rock. Nothing. Meanwhile, we started to see our competition coming, and it was excruciating. We see the boats start to come through, and we thought there's the race, that's done. We ended up getting assistance from the Coast Guard, who brought a small tender out. They leveraged the boat sideways, and then they assisted us to un-wedge ourselves.

We crossed the line and finished, but honestly, because we had rendered outside assistance, we were technically disqualified. So, we ended up crossing the line in fourth, figuratively, but that was our four-peat that never happened. We withdrew from the race due to the penalty. I think what that taught us was you can never take things for granted regardless of the plan that you have and no matter how successful you are. Mother Nature has the final word and the best way of humbling you.

I call that the year on the rocks. Our dock neighbors gave us a little charm. He's a jewelry maker and made a little key chain with a cut out of Graham's shoal, and that is our lucky token. We keep it in the boat, and it makes every trip with us. It's like our voodoo doll, to make sure that we keep the bad spirits away.

100ᵀᴴ ANNIVERSARY OF THE RACE

The next year, 2008, was the hundredth anniversary of the Race to Mackinac. We were game on, and we put a great team together. We prepared all season long, and the boat was in excellent shape, having repaired the damage from the year prior.

We had a great start that year, and we got out far in front of the fleet. We led the fleet the first night. They never saw us after the first night, and we woke up the next morning surrounded by nothing but big boats because we had made it to the larger boat fleet in front of us. We kept on moving, and we ended up winning our section and third overall in the trophy division.

We won two flags that year, a significant accomplishment for the 100th running of the race. Now we had a three-peat, an oops with the rocks, and another win. Next, in 2009, we placed third. We were leading for two-thirds of the race and then lost it in the straights because we got into a drag race where they beat us by going south and catching a better breeze. In 2010, we redeemed ourselves by winning first place again.

2011 was another winning year, very similar to 2008, except that was the year of the Wing Nuts accident. A 38+ knot, gale force storm hit the fleet, and the rain was coming down so hard it hurt your face. We had to use a dive mask while driving in order to see where we were going.

There was lightning, and it was raining sideways when we heard a man overboard and capsized boat called on the radio. I was down below, plotting coordinates for it, to see if we could render assistance, and we decided it was about two-and-a-half miles ahead of us. The boat was named Wing Nuts, and their crew had taken all their sails down. They had pointed their bow into the breeze to survive the storm, and in the process, a wave caught the boat, the boom swung over, and killed two people on their boat instantaneously.

We continued to sail through all of that and put up our storm sail and reduced our sail area on the mainsail. At the time, Wing Nuts was probably two-and-a-half miles in front of us, and by the time we arrived, there were a ton of boats there already, trying to do a search and recovery for the two people who went over. It came out later that they were tethered to the boat and were underneath it.

We won the race that year, but the accident and two people losing their lives understandably overshadowed our win.

PERFORMANCE UNDER PRESSURE

I was vice chair of the Race to Mackinac in 2011, and in 2012 graduated to chairman. That role involved a lot of preparation, and there was a lot of pressure between the planning and running of the race. I was grateful that the Karma team rallied around me to get our boat prepped because I didn't have any extra time. We took fourth place that year, and we still got a plaque, but with all that there was to do, the pressure of leading the race, just finishing was an accomplishment.

We took fourth again in 2013, and I think the distraction of not being able to put my head completely into the race made it very difficult. I'm not a star player, but I think it helps to have everybody engaged. I think that was the biggest lesson I learned those two years, that multitasking is very difficult–seldom are you able to do two things at once, and your attention needs to be solely focused on the race.

In 2014 and 2015, we took first place again, giving us another two-peat. Then we came to 2016 or, as I think of it, the last hurrah and Christina's 25th race. That, of course, is the year that was so difficult due to all that happened with Karma Yacht Sales. We took fourth that year, and it was the last year we raced as a team with the crew that had so many races together.

2017 was the year we chartered a Farr 40 and created a combined program of assorted crew from various boats. It was memorable for many reasons but also because a stormfront crossed the fleet on Saturday causing all sorts of interesting wind and exciting storm conditions. In 2018, I sailed with the boat, Eagle, owned by a fellow Mackinac Committee colleague, Shawn O'Neill and his dad – a historically strong sailing program. We took first place, but it was a nasty year for the weather. There were seven and eight-foot swells and winds between 28 and 32 knots.

That was my ninth win, and the significant part about that one is that my brother and I raced on two different boats, in two different sections, and 331 miles into the race, we ended up racing against each other the final two miles all the way to the finish line.

Marty beat me by about a minute and a half and got his ninth Mac win, and on SV Eagle, we won our section as well, giving me my ninth win, too. It reinforced that building a sailing program is about getting a team together that has a common goal of making the boat go fast. We both lived two examples of that and that supported our experience on our own boat. It gave us hope for the future as we sought to rebuild our program.

SAILING AS A METAPHOR

This made me think back to the years we had Sam on our team and how abused and degraded we felt afterward. Even though we learned a lot from him, it came at a cost—morale. Those last two races aboard Karma ('14 and '15) were without him, it was a pleasure to sail with some really good people and know that while we had learned much from Sam, we did not need him to win.

Over our sailing career, I have had the pleasure of sailing with some amazing sailors- Richard Bouzaid, Volvo Ocean Race (VOR) sailor from Team Alinghi who won the VOR. We sailed with Richard and won our section in the NOOD Regatta. He was our tactician and an amazing sailor who made the boat go phenomenally fast. You walked off the boat and felt great about yourself and your team's performance.

I had the same type of experience with Bill Colombo and Jud Smith when sailing the North Americans, walking off the boat feeling like you learned a lot, and you're a better sailor because you got a chance to sail with them. Much like the many managers I have had the pleasure of working for–I've learned a lot from the great ones, but I've probably learned the most from the ones that were challenged in some form-adversity in a perverse way is sometimes a great teacher of what not to do. Even though you achieve your goal, you understand that there is a better way of going about it.

The sport of sailing is humbling. You could be the best at what you do on land, but you get on the water, and Mother Nature has other plans for you, especially when you're racing one design because all the boats are the same, all the gear is the same, and the sails are the same size. The thing that's different is your plan, your execution of that plan, and your team members and their execution of the plan.

This is an excellent metaphor for business, the systematic process for it. Both are a very interesting ballet. Your foot goes forward, their foot goes back, your foot comes back, and their foot comes forward. The rhythm is all synchronous—in business and on a boat—the epitome of teamwork because doing your job allows somebody else to do theirs.

It's also an outstanding metaphor for life. If we all did our jobs and kept our own things in order, think about how much more productive society would be as opposed to worrying about what others do or passing judgment.

PASSING IT TO THE NEXT GENERATION

I've been fortunate to be able to pass my love for sailing

to both of our daughters. They've both been on sailboats since they were only months old. Formally, they have taken sailing lessons since they were five. They've taken sailing at summer camp, and Sofia, the oldest of the two, left soccer four years ago and decided to dedicate herself full time to sailing. She's now in high school and sails for Saint Ignatius on her high school team.

That's been my pride and joy, watching her develop her own love of the sport and finding her own peace on the water. My wife says, how can you rest—you're always moving sail and other things around, but there's a peacefulness and a calmness that happens on the water. You can have a bad day on land and get on a boat, turn your cell phone off, go out for a sail, and come back. And, for the bit of time that you are on the water, everything gets shut down and goes away. You come back recharged and relaxed.

One of my best days is always a day with the family on the water with Sonia and the girls. Sailing is how my relationship with Sonia began, and now it's come full circle, it is the gift that began so many years ago on Big Blue Lake in Michigan.

CHAPTER 16:

THE ROAD LEAST TRAVELED

"Change is inevitable, but progress is optional."

~ Tony Robbins

It was the fall of 2017, and my career had gone through another evolution that landed me squarely in the tech sector. I had just closed the deal to sell Karma Yacht Sales to Nathan and Susan Randall on September 1st, and had sold off the remaining real estate holdings. This was the moment when you could almost hear the page turning to close that chapter, and the next chapter was ready to be written.

There was a bright white page spread out before me, and all I needed to do was choose my path. As I explored what would be written there, I continued my usual networking through breakfasts and lunches with industry clients and others in the sector. Everyone was always curious to know what I was doing now, how things were with the business, and where I was headed next.

I am grateful to have Thom Dammrich, the president of the National Marine Manufacturers Association (NMMA), as a mentor. He was the gentleman who, in 2015, opened the door for me to step into the Wintrust Board of Directors. I sought him out to be not only a mentor but a sponsor for me in these circles. My interaction with Thom goes back to about 2009 and the depths of the recession when we got industry thought leader groups together to figure out how to get the industry out of the mess it was in.

Thom and I had developed a relationship, not only on the professional level, but he had also been the guy to recommend I join a lot of different boards and committees in the industry. He turned out to be a true sponsor, and to this day, we are still in touch. It's great that even as I write this chapter, I am looking forward to one of our quarterly dinners tonight.

He has since retired from the Wintrust board and the NMMA, but through Thom, I met a variety of different people and built a strong network of professionals and people that know me, know my credibility, and the work that I'd done over the 15 years that I owned Karma Yacht Sales.

BUILD YOUR NETWORK

There's an adage that I believe in and follow. It says you

should build your network before you need it, and I have made it a point to do that. This was one of the times I was transitioning my personal brand away from being a marine boat dealer to what I needed to highlight next.

I learned not to be afraid to use and leverage my network. My network includes those who I'm friends with personally and professionally and others who follow me on social media, including Facebook, Twitter, and LinkedIn. To those people that I mentor, I always ask, "Who are the 10 people that if shit hit the fan, you could call, and they would have your back?"

I know who they are for me. It's my wife, my brother, any of my siblings, my mom, some cousins, and a few professional people that I know I could reach out to. All of them would give it to me straight if I asked them, "Who am I? What's my brand? What am I strong in? What do I suck at?"

Tom is one of those people that, at different points, I've checked in with him. At one of our breakfast meetings, I had shared that I didn't know what to do next. I had an opportunity to invest in a marina, but I had concerns, and, inevitably, it fell apart.

SELF-DISCOVERY, AGAIN

I was struggling with what I wanted to be next. I'd had 15 years of running my own business and being the chief cook and bottle washer. As an entrepreneur, you learn to do a lot of things, even if you might not do them all well—sales, marketing, visionary, and more.

I could start another business, or I could go into something completely different—in another field—but I asked myself, how can I leverage the 15 years I spent in the Marine industry and do something different? I did LOVE the marine industry as it is a fun professional setting.

As I explored my options, I thought about how America's kind of funny because it puts people in buckets. Whenever you talk to people that know brands and teach you how to brand yourself, they don't use their title (a bucket) and instead talk about capabilities (different buckets). I'm a technology executive, Board director, an author, but I'm also a DEI (Diversity, Equity, and Inclusion) advocate and a trailblazer. Those are examples of my personal brand.

So, I went through a self-discovery process where I developed answers to the questions, "What do you really like to do? What does the market need? What am I good at? What can I make money doing?" If you imagine circles with each of those questions and the answers to them. At their intersection is your opportunity-your why. A four-way Venn diagram of sorts.

BEING AN INTRAPRENEUR

I've always been an intrapreneur. That has to do with the way I think about business. I've always thought that whether you're working for an organization, or you own it, you run it as if it was your own business. Even when I was a manager, a product manager, or a national director of sales, I ran my budget as if it was coming out of the Sandoval household budget because I look to maximize ROI (return on investment). How much will the amount spent, bring back in profit and return?

Maybe that's the Latino in me because we're frugal; we're scrappy. We try to make the dollar stretch as far as it'll go. I sometimes think that's a strength and, at other times, a weakness. Some people just don't care, though, and say, "I'm just going to spend the company's money and get the results I get."

I always took extra consideration over the expenditure and asked if I was getting the best value for the dollar. I think that's part of what made me functionally successful as an entrepreneur because I was already prepping for that when I was working for a large Fortune 100 company. I was good at business operations and developing a brand into what it needed to be. I took a brand that was relatively unknown, and we created Karma Yacht Sales. Who the hell names a business Karma and then turns it into a national brand and one of the top three dealers in the network and North America?

I was particularly good at branding, leveraging resources, and bringing people together to achieve results.

AN ENTREPRENEUR IN CORPORATE MODE

As I continued to explore my capabilities and search for my next path, I also started to think about what my non-negotiables were. I needed to be in a place that let me continue to flex my entrepreneurial muscle, and that's very difficult to do inside corporate because they put you in a box and say you have to fit in here, you have to do what the job title says. This is your lane, and you have to stay in it. Don't break the rules.

Guys like me end up running their own business, and they don't often go back the other way, but I thought there's something else here to learn. So, back to my breakfast with Thom. He mentioned some colleagues at Brunswick Corporation, reminding me that I had been on a couple of boards with a few of the executives and a task force with others. He advised that there might be some synergy with some projects they were working on. In fact, I would later learn of a new product where they were starting to use technology to better connect their products with their end consumers and develop a better customer experience for them.

This spoke to me because I had leveraged technology to build a system that connected our cash payment system, our CRM, and our dealer management network to improve our end user experience at KYS. It's what led to improving our customer satisfaction index to 100 percent. Since learning how to code during my undergrad years, I've embraced the geek and techy side of me.

I sent one of the execs a text, and he quickly put me in touch with a couple of people on the leadership team that I could talk to about the company. I think the question on their end was, "All right, he's done really well as an entrepreneur, but how would he fit going back the other way? How does that look? How does that work out?"

Corporations are very risk-averse when they get to a certain level and are publicly traded. Bringing somebody on at that level, in that capacity, is risky, but from what I could glean in a conversation with their CEO, this was an interesting new venture. They had started it from an innovation fund and were trying to use disruptive innovation to fundamentally change the trajectory of their business.

Typical product development has you develop a product inside the umbrella of the company, and within that umbrella, they tell you how to do things–A, then B, then C, so you follow a waterfall mechanism. And the way that they were doing it was following a methodology called agile, which emanates from the customer pain point. It is the application of insights stemming from customer empathy to solve a problem–the why.

It asks what is the pain to the customer? What is the need? What is your why? What are you fulfilling? The pain was the difficulty for new and experienced boaters to be able to connect with their device, to stay ahead of the maintenance items that needed to get done, but also develop a strong connection to the brand for the purposes of the longevity of the brand.

I talked to the leader on the technical side and the GM of the group. They told me a little about the company culture, and I shared my background. I positioned my personal business plan for how I would go-to-market. Ironically, they would later share that it was spot on with theirs, so there was immediate alignment. The day I met with them, I finished the discussion at the loop lab and went to my car to think through the discussion and take some notes while the thoughts were fresh in my mind. As I looked at the date, October 19, 2017—it dawned on me that just one year prior, I was sitting in my dad's doctor's office learning that he had a limited time to live. The significance of that moment did not escape me. Perhaps it was Dad's way of showing me that this was the path for now.

I had always admired Brunswick Corp. as being one of the top companies. There are two companies that are formidable in the Marine industry, Brunswick on one side and Beneteau on the other. If I was going to go to a company that matched the level of market leadership that I had been a part of, then there was only going up, not down or backwards. So, the answer was clear.

When I think of this, I go back to the conversation with my grandmother after I had decided not to go to med school. I had laid all the decisions and options out for her, and she asked me what I was going to do. I told her I had a plan. She said, "You always have a plan, but what are you going to do? There is only one way, and that's forward and upwards."

ON A MISSION

With her words ringing in my ears, the offer was formalized and we agreed I would come on board the Brunswick team. I had a strong admiration for all the people that I interacted with at Brunswick, what they were capable of doing, and the market share that they built in the industry for all their brands. What better company was there to do this? They had this satellite location called the Loop Lab downtown, which was right off Wacker Drive on Adams. It provided just enough distance from the corporate headquarters, but a sense of connection that helped us with visibility but did not impede our autonomy. Each member of the team was handpicked for the ability to be a self-starter and work with ample autonomy to build and create.

We started out in a little 950 square foot office and later moved to a larger one. We also started out with a six-person team, set all the major capabilities, and each one of these people were A-list players that were self-starters like me.

If you're going to build a business from scratch, you need people that see the mission of where you're going and want to get there fast. They make decisions quickly. They have networks, they have resources, and they can move on a decision quickly. We were innovative and each person was not hung up on titles, because we all shared in the success.

We were a really young and scrappy team, and we developed an MVP that was tested in the market for market fit. Then we went with version 1.0, took that out to market, and got some traction early on.

If you put that exact organization inside a large company, it might not do as well because you would be taking very empowered, very entrepreneurial, very driven individuals and putting them in a box that could throttle back on innovation. So, that six-person team accomplished what it took divisions of 3,000 people five to ten years to build.

We built the brand from scratch. We built a market presence. We took it on a roadshow to test and, using very nimble, agile methodology, entered a cycle of continually iterating and improving it as time went on.

During the first year, we launched the software, the hardware, and the UI, the user interface. It was three products in one—there was a software part, the interface portal, and then there was the backend, which was tied to the hardware that went on the boats. The user interface, which was an app for your smart device, allowed you to connect to the boat remotely.

The hardware went on the boat and sent information from the boat to the interface on the computer portal and on your app. This way, you could get information from your boat without having to be not on it. The same way that today you can get from the app for your car or with Nest for your home.

In year two, I could see the change coming. The corporation gave us the money to run with, to get it started, and then they started to pull back some of those controls, the latitude, the entrepreneurialism, and the empowerment. There were a lot of things that could have been done differently during that second year. There were many lessons that we learned, some by winning, and some by failing.

NO MORE STARTUP

Maybe that was the greenness of our team or a little bit of our naivete, but near the end of year two, we saw the exit of our general manager, and then they rolled us into another division the next year.

But that first year was amazing. We were on a learning curve, on the way up, and excited because every day is a new day. I put in many miles of travel in that first year and a half, constantly out talking to customers and different people, and as one of the key advisors helping to build the brand, I was working with our marketing director, our GM, and our tech team.

Year three is when they put us inside a division where we didn't seem to fit. We knew that there had to be a greater plan, but it wasn't readily apparent to us. Communications became more siloed. We were reporting directly to another manager, and that made the experience very challenging. A couple of people left the team to go to other opportunities inside the company, and some of us persevered and continued to press on. I had served as the front face of the business to the industry—good, bad, or indifferent, that was my role.

That was one of the main reasons I was brought on board, to develop and build those industry connections with the product.

HELLO COVID

It was now year three and the beginning of 2020. We started the year at the consumer electronics show in Las Vegas, showcasing what we had built alongside other products from the company.

I got there on Monday and immediately got sick. I might have even had Covid because I felt miserable, sneezing and coughing, and I stayed in my room because I felt horrible. I rallied and eventually left on Friday.

The following week, I needed to be in Seattle for a meeting but was so sick that I went back to my hotel room and got under the covers for an hour. I rallied enough for a dinner meeting but was not my usual self.

I went home, called my doctor, and he said I had the flu and should stay home for as long as needed to rest up, work remotely, and do everything I could to get better. This was in mid to late February. While antigen testing showed otherwise, I'm convinced that I had covid during that bout of the flu. It added to the disconnection from the project that seemed to be transitioning in front of us.

THE REORGANIZATION

Ultimately, our group was placed inside of a new division that was created. In a typical M&A- type structure, our team was integrated into other matrixed roles. Code for some of us were absorbed and others were not. I happened to be in the latter category.

However difficult, the reorganization served as a liberation of sorts. I truly loved my time working there, and I learned a lot. I had the utmost regard for all the people that I worked with and the individuals that I connected with and mentored.

THE END OF A GREAT RUN

I had some pretty good heart to hearts discussions with some of the leadership there, and they said, "You could probably do any job here at the company. You're a very talented individual, but is this what you really want to do?" Whether they were placating me or not, I had to do some soul searching on that and decided the best thing to do might be to walk away, at least for now. So, I ended that chapter.

WHAT I LEARNED

I learned a lot about myself there in these three years—what I liked and what I didn't like, where I was strong and where I was not so strong, and then also I learned about what I wanted moving forward.

I did a lot of soul searching and started consulting a little bit with clients and people that I knew in the industries of healthcare and technology. I wasn't afraid to work hard, roll-up my sleeves and jump into it. It signaled just another transition point in my life.

The progress for me came in my evolution of struggle–the ability to not pay it mind and move on to what was next. One of the tales of the Grumpy Grandma that I heard from my abuelita growing up, was that sometimes when one door closes, another opens. Perhaps this was not for me, yet put in my path so that I might learn. Time would be the ultimate teacher in that.

CHAPTER 17:

BECOMING THE SIXTY-NINTH

"You Can Recognize a Pioneer by The Arrows in His Back." ~ Beverly Rubik

Chicago is the city of many borders and divisions--North Side, South Side, East Side, West Side, Brownsville, Wrigleyville, Pilsen, Bucktown, Rogers Park, White Sox, Cubs. There are more than I can list here.

The Chicago that I grew up in, the South Side of Chicago, was a stone's throw away from the North Side. I still remember the very first time that I realized that. I took a train downtown with my grandfather, and the whole world, the downtown area, was vastly different from the neighborhood I grew up in.

My neighborhood had a nice thriving commercial district because it was a central area for a lot of working-class people, but it was remarkably different from the loop, where you saw people walking around in suits, hustling and bustling to their jobs.

My next foray into the North Side life was when I went for my undergrad degree at DePaul, and I commuted my first year. I had to drive to DePaul through this area where you couldn't go south of Webster because the neighborhood was still in transition from a mostly Puerto Rican neighborhood to a more gentrified community.

In the early eighties, you couldn't leave your car parked there for too long, or you would come back and find your windows broken. There were a lot of vacant houses where drug addicts lived, and needles were all over. This was Lincoln Park (South of Armitage) back in the day, and it was a mess.

Then as the neighborhood transformed and people bought up the properties and turned them into nice single-family homes and apartments, the property values all around DePaul skyrocketed. I would walk down some of the streets there and look around me in awe, thinking, "Wow, people live like this."

It was a whole different lifestyle than the one I knew, especially as a kid that grew up in a mostly working-class community in the shadows of the steel mills.

BUYING A BOAT

In 1997, when we bought Chiquita, our little 26-foot AMF yellow Paceship with the ugly brown plaid, it was a way to get out on the water and engage in something that we hadn't grown up doing. We were four guys from the Southeast Side that grew up in working-class families that cobbled their money together to buy a $7,800, 20+-year-old boat.

We just wanted to get out on the water, and we did that. We sailed a vast 52 days in our inaugural season, 52+ trips, and we diligently logged each one of them in our ships' log, adding a few words to what we were doing that day and what the experience was like. I still have that log, and it's a neat thing to look at from time to time and think about how it all started.

There wasn't a day we couldn't sail. Our boat was moored in Monroe Harbor on mooring ball NU26. It was in the north knuckle of Monroe Harbor, close to the sea wall, a short distance away from Columbia Yacht Club, which was kind of a folksy yacht club—a ferry boat that was turned into a private yacht club. Just south and west of us, adjacent to the tender launch for Monroe Harbor, and adjacent to the public dock and pump out was the Chicago Yacht Club.

It was a gleaming glass building with a parking lot, its own docks, and at that time, it had a gas dock. We had ventured into the Chicago Yacht Club a few times as guests of members, and then we had gone to the public Friday Mac party every year that we could. We experienced it from that perspective, and one day we were waiting for some people to go sailing. And as I was sitting there enjoying a cigar, I looked over and wondered how to become a member.

JOINING THE CLUB

I decided to walk over and find out. So, I walked over to the front desk and was greeted immediately by a guard. He asked what I was doing there, and I explained that I wanted to learn a little bit more about the club. I went and talked to the attendant, who introduced me to the membership director, a young lady by the name of Christy.

She talked to me a little bit about the yacht club and gave me a very quick tour around. I told her that I didn't know anybody there that was a member. She said she could help me with that and was able to set up a meeting with one person as a sponsor and two others as endorsers.

I remember not knowing what to wear to the meeting, so I wore a suit jacket with a tie and khakis. I ended up meeting with Pete Styles, Greg Freeman, and Bonnie Barski. The questions were pretty simple—why you're interested in boating, do you own a boat, what do you plan on doing, what do you want to do long term —the typical questions.

I told them my boat was nothing fancy and described it to them. Our crew was waiting for me to finish this meeting so we could go sailing, and I pointed to it. These guys all had had very beautiful boats that were easily double or triple the size of my boat, and definitely more expensive.

I remember them asking me, do you own the boat by

yourself? I said, no, I own it with three other guys, and they asked if they would all be coming into the club. I said they probably would if that was allowed. They commented that they needed to be clear—it's not one guy who buys a membership, and everybody uses it.

I said, "Oh, I understand that." I went through the rest of the process and had my admission luncheon. They asked me some of the same questions I had been asked at the first meeting, and as part of the application, I had to write an essay on why I wanted to join the club. The advice that I was given by the three people who had interviewed me the first time–because they had become my proxies and mentors–was that I would be fine.

I remember talking to an older gentleman, Commodore Parks, a very prestigious gentleman. He had been a Commodore of the club and was also a recognized Olympic sailor and world champion in one of the sailboat classes. He was very nice in talking to me and made me feel very welcome.

I went through the rest of the evening, joined, and officially got my acceptance right before the 4th of July 1999, which was perfect because I wanted to go to their 4th of July party. Fast forward, and I'm now going into my 23rd year of membership. It sure is funny how time flies.

I joined as an associate, which was for people below the age of 40. I immediately got active in the associate's committee, which was an affable group of young people all about my age. We got together, had a lot of parties, and hung out. One of the guys on the committee, Jim Armstrong, told me that if I wanted to get the most out of the club, I should volunteer, get into the community of the club, and get to know people.

GETTING INVOLVED

I took his advice and joined him on the sponsorship committee. We worked on sponsorship for all the club events, but mostly for the Race to Mackinac. My first luxurious assignment in the sponsorship committee was to put up LaSalle Bank banners on the pilings. Being the young guy and the new kid on the block, you get the grunt work. As promised, a great way to meet people.

In talking to LaSalle Bank about sponsorship, they suggested it would be great if we could hold more events that drew on-land engagement for the Mac race. I knew some people at Navy Pier and talked to them about our idea. We put together a plan where Navy Pier would provide, or we would rent, a simple stage with some chairs and a microphone, and we would have a parade of boats, and as the boat went by, we would announce who was on each boat and call out to them as they passed.

Sponsorship ran that for a few years, and it continued to grow in popularity each year, so we decided to bring it in under the Race to Mackinac committee umbrella, and that became my entry onto the Mac committee.

At that time, I was also on the membership and sponsorship committees, but the Mac committee is the queen committee of the whole club. We plan the race for 12 months and enjoy the race for one week at a budget of several million. When you are a part of the planning and operations of the race, you get to understand what a significant operation it is to run each year, and it's mostly done by volunteers.

There are thousands of volunteer hours that go into that event, from the race committee all the way to organizing things and working with club staff to deliver what is needed. Bringing the boat parade under the Mac committee and branding it under the Race to Mackinac was my first assignment.

The first guy that I worked with at the Mac committee was Rick Lillie, a really nice gentleman who I am still friends with to this day. I had the benefit of serving with Rick, who was our secretary for two terms while I was vice commodore and then Commodore. What I love about Rick is that he epitomized servant leadership.

There was no job that Rick wasn't willing to volunteer for, roll up his sleeves, and get done. From a mentorship standpoint, I idolized Rick a lot for who he was as a steward of service. He was all about service, and a lot of how I had been brought up was focusing on being of service.

I started on the committee in 2004 and was on the committee for seven years, through a couple of chairmen, and no one ever approached me about being Mac chair. I was the steady Eddie guy. I knew how the committee worked and how the entire race operated from being on the committee all those years.

In typical Latino fashion, I didn't advocate for myself. I just showed up and did the work, figuring that sooner or later, somebody would notice me. I had a lot of opportunities to grow in that job under the Mac chair for 2008, Greg Miarecki. I ran the PR and the branding and marketing initiatives for the 2008 race, which was our hundredth running of the race. In that particular race, we sold out and had 435 boats that participated in the event, where we normally had 300 boats.

It was a massive success for a significant milestone. That also happened to be the year that I placed in a double win for our boat. Just as important to me was the ability to work on a team that was very collaborative, and a lot of credit for that goes to Greg. There were a lot of things I learned from him, and I noticed a lot of the great things that he did for the club and still does today.

BECOMING CHAIRMAN

My chance to step into a position on the committee came in 2011 when Greg Freeman, my endorser when I joined, was ready to hand chairman of the Mac committee to his vice-chairman after the normal two-year period. As it turned out, his vice-chairman decided to move and could no longer step into the position of chairman.

That two years as vice-chairman helped with the transference of knowledge, and the gap could be a challenge for the committee. At first, the plan was for me to step into vice chairman for a year and have Greg stay for a third year, and then I would take over as chairman. I was ambivalent about jumping right into the chairman position, and a lot of that was self-doubt and my lack of confidence. I knew everything I needed to know to run the race, and a lot of it is institutionalized, but I was very hesitant to take it out of respect for Greg.

Understandably, Greg had gotten the impression that he was going to go for the third year, but the immediate past chairman on the committee and Rear Commodore oversees appointing the next chairman. Then, the 2011 race took place, and that was the year we lost two people in the Wing Nuts accident.

They ended up deciding that I would take over as chairman, keeping Greg to the normal two-year period. So, in 2012 I became chairman of the Mac committee and was voted onto the Board of Directors for the club. Historically, the Mac chairman had a seat on the board, and it was also an opportunity to be part of the leadership of the club.

Being the Mac chair for two years, 2012 and 2013, was really challenging because racing is an all-hands-on deck thing, and being one of the owners of the boat and the guy that did a lot of the coordination, meant that our team had to step up and fill in the gaps because I was busy running the race up until the moment that I stepped onto the boat on Saturday morning.

It was very busy, so those two years we didn't do so great. I think we took a third and a fourth those two years. Obviously, my mind was not in the game. I was distracted, especially in 2012, because it was the first year after the accident, and I was busy getting the race back on track, getting people's confidence up, executing the plan, and helping them to see that it was going to be safe.

We put a strategic plan together for getting it back on track, and we made some changes and implementations following the investigation of the 2011 race by the governing body of the sport. It was a big pivot point for the race. I stepped in, and we did fantastically the next year; the planning helped contain any drop in participation and minimize it.

A BALANCING ACT

I did two years, and I learned a lot and had a lot of fun. It was very difficult for me, though, as I had to balance my crew and my business. I was running the business at the time we were trying to recover from the recession. And then, I still had two daughters that were very young, and Sonia had just gone back to work in 2011.

I guess I've always been one of those people that the way I get things done is by being under a bit of pressure. There's a saying, "If you want to get something done, give it to a busy person." That seems to be me.

THE ROAD TO COMMODORE

After I was done as Mac chairman, I stayed on the committee for one more year to make sure the transference to the guy behind me was strong, and then in 2014, I was nominated to the flag, or executive committee of the club, to the position of Rear Commodore who oversees 18 on the water committees such as the regattas, the junior program, and anything that happens on the water. You could call him the de facto operations guy.

Those two years were difficult because I was being torn between the challenges with my business and my club life. And then, I'm being asked to serve and stay committed as Rear Commodore. I was almost living two lives during that period of time there, and I had to pull back a little bit to balance things out. Something was going to give; I was under a lot of stress, but I needed to continue to deliver within my business.

Added to it was the sense of commitment because the commitment includes two years as Rear Commodore, two years as Vice Commodore, and then two years as Commodore. Once you're on that trajectory, you've got a six-year commitment. It gave me flashbacks to climbing Mt. Rainier when you look back to see how far you've come, but then you still see how far you've got to go, and you think, "Do I really want to make the climb?" I think there were times when I thought that I bit off more than I could chew.

The pandemic hit halfway through my term as Commodore, which challenged us when it came to our usual revenue operations because we had to cancel many major events, which were a large source of revenue. It was then that having an agile mindset, the same thing I had used with the startup at Brunswick, helped me to put new building blocks in place with the goal of reopening the club and getting our revenue stream restarted.

We were flexible and evolved quickly. As requirements shifted, so did we. We sent messages to the club members, letting them know the club was open and they would be safe; that we had safety measures in place. We brought air purifiers in, and the whole plan was to make everybody feel comfortable. We owe many thanks to all our members--they supported the club amazingly that year. They came back, they felt safe, and they used it. Through teamwork, perseverance and a lot of prayers we turned a large six figure deficit at the end of Q2 into finishing the year in the black.

A TIME OF CIVIL UNREST

Then there was the aspect of civil unrest and going through two different worlds. Here I am, a person of color, with my feet in two buckets. I'm straddling two worlds—one where I'm negotiating the reopening of the harbors and people are complaining because they can't get their boats into the harbor. They couldn't go out and use their boats and be free and do what they felt they had the privilege to do.

Then, at the same time, we're fielding calls from my family where I'm getting reports of friends and family who came down with Covid, and we're trying to keep my mother-in-law from coming down with Covid, too.

I remember having a dialogue with Mayor Lori Lightfoot at one point, and I said, "I know what you're going through. You're trying to do the right thing for the city, and it's a thankless job because any decision you make is going to be a battle." That's the crux of leadership; your job is to decide, and either way, you need to understand that somehow, somewhere, people are going to be unhappy with your decision.

I've always believed that you're better off if both sides dislike you because at least you know you're doing something. You'll die trying to please them all, so you just have to make a decision.

At that time, we had a very capable general manager of the club, but not the most innovative person. He was a guy that showed up and did his job but wasn't very good at making decisions. He was the antithesis of me and would drag on and procrastinate at times. We worked around that as a team though to support each other.

My wife will tell you I'm extremely decisive. I see black and white, but I don't see gray at times. Sometimes that's a strength, and sometimes it's a weakness. In situations of crisis, and through the training that I've had as an EMT, you learn to be very decisive and get into action because that's what you're charged with doing.

EXPERIENCES MATTER

In large part, my experiences as a member of the Chicago Yacht Club have been great. I have many people at the club that we care dearly for–strong acquaintances that we see on a regular basis and a few friends. It is the place that our daughters have grown up at and feel comfortable going to.

I've had a number of experiences throughout my life that were due to my skin color, and although I'd hoped to be free of those at the club, I suppose I wasn't surprised that they happened there, too. There is a saying that just because you are "in the club," does not mean that you are really "in the club." Differences matter to some.

The first time, I was a club member for almost a month. And I remember the day because I had driven down from work in the north suburbs. I was hustling to park my car in the parking lot at the club so that we could go sailing, and I realized I had on a button-down collar dress shirt. So, I went to the front desk at the club and bought a sports shirt that was similar to what the staff would wear. It was a white shirt with the club logo on it.

I'm sitting down, waiting for the people that I was going to meet with—a committee meeting of some sort. I went to the bar to get a drink, and this older gentleman, who was sitting at a table, signaled me over, and he asked me to get him a drink. I wasn't sure if there was a hazing of new members where you had to buy older guys a drink or something, so I said, "Buy you a drink?"

He says no, just get me a drink on my member number. I'm paying for it. Of course, I was a little slow to catch on. Suddenly, I realized he confused me for somebody that worked at the club because you didn't see a lot of Hispanics in the yacht club. My brother and I are probably two of the more visible people there, and we've got a few others, but most of our wait staff is Hispanic and that is what some members are used to.

TOUGH DECISIONS

One of the biggest challenges that I had to face during the pandemic was deciding who to furlough. I'm looking at the names of 76 people we had to furlough, and all I remember saying to the general manager was, I have to make sure that their health benefits are covered during the period that we have to furlough them.

It really weighed on me that I had to be the first Hispanic Commodore at the Chicago Yacht Club to make the decision to furlough mostly black and brown people that worked at the club. It was really difficult for me to do—a true crux of leadership.

I remember Sonia saying, how can you sleep? I told her the decision had to be made. You can't just pay people indefinitely to sit at home. It was my fiduciary responsibility, but it conflicted with my humanity. You realize that behind every one of those names is a family, a household. There are people that depend on them.

PROUD MOMENTS

I remember the day that I was nominated as Commodore, and I remember one of our Hispanic wait staff coming up to me, and he actually made me cry. He comes up and says, "I was going to retire, but now I want to wait until after you are done. I want to be able to tell my children that I served and worked under the very first Hispanic Commodore at the Chicago Yacht Club."

It made me think of all my relatives who have worked

in service jobs. This gentleman just retired on January 1st. I've proudly written a lot of letters of recommendation for the kids of our staff members to get into college, to go to DePaul, Loyola, and Northwestern. They come to me and say, "I want my children to meet you because you are what we want them to be."

What an honor. You feel the weight of being the very first of anything because you can't screw up. If you do, it's screwed up for anybody else behind you. There's a different lens on you as the first and definitely more pressure.

HATE MAIL AND THE HUMAN CONDITION

I wrote a Commodore's letter once about the social unrest that was going on and about how our community was so blessed, so privileged, and how it was incumbent upon us to be aware of the impression we make in the city. For that, I got hate mail from people saying, "Don't be proselytizing. I don't come to the club for your politics."

I said this isn't political; this is a human condition. You know, we are very blessed, and to whom much is given, much is expected. There were some people that could not understand that.

We do a survey every year at the club toward the end of the year, and as Commodore, you get to see the raw numbers and the feedback. I remember at the end of 2019 we did our first survey of my first term. That year, there were people that wrote, I can't wait 'til we're done with this social experiment of this Latino Commodore, this immigrant

Commodore. I thought, wow, that's ugly. It wasn't a lot of people, but a select few.

I knew that when I gave my address for the first annual meeting that I did in November 2019, my wife had some people sitting behind her, and they were talking under their breath about, "There he goes with his diversity bullshit," because I actually called them all out on it.

I said that as a club, we are better than this. I think a lot of people were shocked that I called them out on the fact that they would put something like that in a survey. Another one had read, "Illegal Commodore, let's get a real yachtsman, not somebody that's a poser.

I remember talking to other Commodores, asking if they ever got that kind of hate mail. And they said they got hate mail but had never seen it that bad. It was horrible. I shared it with our board. I shared it with the club at that meeting. There were a lot of people who said, "That is not our club. Those people should be outed and kicked out of the club."

I remember my daughters being in the audience, and on the ride home, we talked about it, and they asked, "Dad, how does that make you feel?" It meant that I was in the right spot, because if it's not me, then who?

It's an undertone because you're breaking barriers, and people are uncomfortable. They're uncomfortable with the fact that you're there. I remember telling everybody at the club, "I don't derive my value as a person by what people here think of me. I have a lot of people that I like here and a lot of alliances, but the people that I respond to are the people that I eat dinner with on a regular basis, my family that I'm responsible for."

From a cultural perspective, our family is tight, and my extended family is tight. My brother is my best friend. We have dinner with our kids and families at the club. We sit together, but for many of the people at the club, their kids are off the school, and their friends are at the club. That's who their community is. For us, not so much because I remember the value system my dad raised me with. It's family first, then friends, and then everything else. It doesn't make us better; it just makes us different.

OATMEAL AND AN ATTITUDE

Another episode happened on St. Patrick's Day 2019. I was shooting a video for my vlog that I was doing as Commodore, trying a different way to communicate with people. On my way back into the building, I see a man who I served with on the membership committee many years ago, and he says, "Can you get me some milk for my oatmeal?" I told him sure, I would have the staff get him that. The man became quite aggressive and insisted that he wanted me to get the milk for his freaking oatmeal.

I thought, here we go. How far have we come? I am the first Hispanic Commodore in 145 years of a club that is one of the top 25 clubs in the world. I've been a member here for 21 years, and this man knows who I am and the insult he is delivering on purpose.

I have been, and will continue to be, the biggest defender

of our staff. I cannot stand people who treat others that way. I don't care who they are.

For most of my life, I have walked the path least traveled, and my role as the sixty-ninth commodore of the Chicago Yacht Club was just that. Many might cringe when I say that I am the first Hispanic commodore of the club, however it is a sense of pride that resonates in a city whose population is almost 38 percent Hispanic. Toward the end of my term, one of the local news channels did a story on the historic significance of my term as commodore.

The story reached a very wide audience, and the overall response was positive. It was reported to me that there were 1.9 million impressions, and a ridiculous number of shares of the online story were made. The news reporter that did the story, a Latina herself, was proud to do the story because we often don't hear about the successes (albeit as small as mine) in our community.

It's not like I cured cancer, however for some children out there, it might just be the thing that piques their interest and they take to the water much like I did many years ago.

That would make my journey down the path least traveled worthwhile.

CHAPTER 18

THE PIVOT

"Your time is limited, so don't waste it living someone else's life. Don't be trapped by dogma – which is living with the results of other people's thinking. Don't let the noise of other's opinions drown out your own inner voice. And most important, have the courage to follow your heart and intuition. They somehow already know what you truly want to become. Everything else is secondary."

~ Steve Jobs

For those of us who lived through it, the year 2020 challenged us all, personally, and professionally. It was the year Covid-19 began, when the pandemic started, when toilet paper was hard to come by, and more people lost their jobs or worked from home than at any time in recent history.

For me, the start-up rollercoaster ride ended in 2020. I finished up my time with Brunswick, said goodbye to the innovative corporate startup that we had grown over three years, and set out to see what was next for me.

My time there had more highs than lows, and we worked at a fast pace because we were excited to be building something new. Then there was the period where it was moved into business acceleration and the start of integration into a traditional business unit. We were rolled up into a new division, and that was where it ended for me.

As I left Brunswick and entered the pandemic, I saw more clearly how we were challenged career wise and socially. The isolation, the constant strife, the stress, and the fear--it was difficult. On top of that, I had just finished my two years as Commodore at the Chicago Yacht Club, and that had exhausted me mentally and physically.

THE STRUGGLE IS REAL

I was given the time to think about many situations that I had encountered. Mirrored by the issues of the world around us, I was able to reflect on my experience of the past few years. I learned a lot, but some of my experiences and feelings of isolation were tough. It's hard to feel like I'm the only one of my kind in an industry that seemed like it didn't want to appeal to one of the largest and fastest growing demographics with $1.7 billion in buying power.

Was it for me? I was tired of being the poster child for diversity. I had carried that mantle for some time in the marine industry and nothing had changed. What was it all for?

Very present for me was the struggle that employees of color face inside companies where they were one of the few. The George Floyd riots and upwelling over an issue that had been swept under the carpet for so many years expanded the conversation and awareness of privilege and the inequities in American society. My own experience as the first Hispanic commodore of a 145-year-old institution was also weighing on me, and it seemed like no one cared.

During my time in corporate America, the obvious truth would sting—true inclusion of all types was lacking. Perhaps that is why such a large percentage of employees eventually leave companies and set out on their own. While conversing with other Hispanic employees that I mentored, they would speak the reality that I had lived during my lifetime. There is much mentoring inside large corporations and little connection with who the individuals really are. The need for a Latino to leave their culture at the door–suppress it, contain it–leads to unhappiness. It leads to a feeling that there is no inclusion at all. That who we fundamentally are does not matter. That our values do not matter.

One conversation really made me think. It was with a very talented employee with stellar educational credentials. We had taken on a mentor/mentee relationship. Over time, our conversations covered the challenges he encountered in his project management roles. He was in the leadership program at the company, and he shared that it seemed at times, like he was always getting the 'crappy projects,' the ones no one wanted.

It seemed to him that other, white employees would push

back on the assignments that they did not like and receive accommodations. Yet, he was told to stick to his project and deliver. He would deliver to the highest degree, but it never seemed like enough. On top of that, he was lonely and uninspired by his work. One day, he shared that he had received an offer from a company in a different field. It looked stimulating and he felt that he could learn a lot.

However, he was conflicted because he felt a sense of loyalty to the company. After much discussion, my advice to him was that he needed to do what was best for him. I would miss him, but it would not end our business relationship. I think he just needed validation that he was founded in his thoughts. His heart was already guiding him to make the right decision.

He also shared how loneliness affected him. He said, "Aside from you, there are few other Latinos in the company. You are the most visible. It is sad that I wait to see the housekeeping team when I work late here, so that I can speak Spanish with them and miss home and my community less." Our lack of representation matters.

Stories like those speak to a need that we have in corporate America. Less than four percent of corporate employees are Hispanic. Even more disturbing is that those numbers seem to be going in the wrong direction. The lack of inclusion, and the failed attempts to create cultures where people feel like they belong, is negatively impacting this statistic. Perhaps that is one of the key reasons so many of us leave corporations to build our own businesses, because it is in those businesses that we can mold the culture that helps us thrive.

I have so many things in my head–experiences, microaggressions, and injustices–that I have experienced in my life. I never wanted to single myself out as Hispanic for fear that I might be cast aside, that I might be cut from the team. I learned to suppress it–to code switch, and it was eating at me.

I had so many thoughts and journaling alone, a mechanism to capture those thoughts and soothe me, was no longer enough. I was tired of being tired.

APPLYING WHAT I HAD LEARNED

I was unsure of what the future held, and I needed to clear my head. I really needed to get away from things, but we were in the middle of a pandemic and the kids were going to school remotely. It wasn't a great time to do that. Thank God we had the financial resources for me to be able to take my time as I conducted a job search because it wasn't going to happen overnight.

We hunkered down and were ready for however long it took.

I kept asking Sonia to allow me to take a sabbatical. I'd envisioned a trip out west where I just jumped in the truck and drove out west and drove through the mountains and Zion National Park and all these different places—to do my own version of Thelma and Louise. Not off the edge of the Grand Canyon but stopping just short of the climax moment.

Instead, because I needed to keep my mind busy, I took the time to take stock of the technical aptitude that

I had built over the previous three years, and I started doing some gap consulting for some clients that needed contactless payment systems or ordering systems built for their businesses. This process of building things was therapeutic for me.

I built a couple of those, and the money was pretty good. I led with the minimum viable product and the version 1.0, which made it very lucrative. It was fun, and now I could start to see the value of what I had gone through with Brunswick. I learned the development of the product from a very basic level. Obviously there the application was Marine, but now I was able to apply it to another area—food and beverage as well as consumer goods.

SELF-REFLECTION

That felt to me like the pivot point, where I went back to the lessons from my dad—that when you work hard and apply yourself, you will never go hungry. This was just another chapter in my life, and now this book.

Finally, a few days after Thanksgiving, I had a conversation with Sonia and I said, "Listen, I really need to get away and clear my head. I want to start the new year with a clean slate. I can't have this fogginess in my head, this self-doubt, this criticism of myself." When you come upon an ending like that, or a failure, it's easy to blame yourself for the things you didn't do right. Perhaps you could have done better.

So, five days before Christmas I decided to jump in a car, go to Michigan, and rent a place. I took a stack of journals, some books, and some things to listen to on my phone so I could clear my head and meditate. I brought some cigars and a couple bottles of bourbon, and I just sat around and journaled and read and meditated about what I wanted in my life, what I was good at, what I needed in the future and what I saw as possibilities. I took some long hikes in the woods. Being alone in the quite woods was soothing. It was serene. It was serene. I could be alone with my thoughts— seek clarity.

When I started looking back on my life, it became clear to me—I like to build companies. I like to build teams and I like to build high performing brands. That was my history, so when I really looked at what I needed, I needed some place where I could do that and leave a legacy.

I needed to feel that validation, in some shape or fashion. I remember the day. It was at sunset, after a long hike that I took on the lakefront in Holland, Michigan. I was making my way back to Ottawa Beach State Park, where I had parked my car. The sun was starting to go down over the lake and I sat on top of one of the sand dunes. The winds were whipping around, and I wrote down what I wanted to declare.

MY DECLARATION

That declaration said I wanted an opportunity to build, to leave a legacy and create something meaningful. I took that, folded it into a square, burned it with a lighter, and let it go into the air. As it drifted away, I went back and did some more journaling and meditating before heading home.

A couple of days after Christmas, I got a call from a colleague and asked me to look at something as though I was an investor. He said, "I know this isn't in your wheelhouse, but I think that given your background of having navigated the yacht club through all its challenges, this might be another challenge you're up for."

He sent me a pitch deck. I took a look at it because I was curious. It was a company named SupplyHive, an odd name for a company. It was in the B2B software business and the company had created a software platform to manage suppliers and the companies that bought products or services from them.

I met virtually with Matt Randal and asked if he could share the financials, because I would like to learn more. He agreed, and it was an interesting company. Their founder, Mark Orgullo had developed the company in 2018 and was the second company in this space that he had started. He had exited the first company when he sold it to a private equity firm.

He was an interesting, visionary guy and a category leader in this space of supplier diversity, performance management, and procurement. My first question to Matt and another angel investor I met with was, does Mark know about this? I was told yes, and that Mark didn't want to be the CEO.

Then they added, "Oh, by the way, we're also bringing on a new chairman of the board." I asked to meet him, and we spent a couple of hours talking. Jeremiah was steeped in wisdom and a genuine salt-of-the-earth kind of gentleman. We hit it off right away and began to develop trust in each other.

THE SUPPLYHIVE COMEBACK

SupplyHive began in 2018 and saw noteworthy success in the year 2020. While most companies were sent into a tailspin by the pandemic, the capable and scrappy team at SupplyHive was able to transition a product offering from a minimum viable product into a solid version 1.0. This was a significant success by a resourceful and small team who also successfully secured seven well-known Fortune 100 clients with a total contract value of over a million dollars a year. This came while persevering through some interesting internal challenges due to the eccentric and unorthodox leadership of the founder.

During this time, the original two angel investors lost confidence in the founder and started leaning into the company, getting involved in operations. This created a bit of a mess marked by tactical decisions made with what appeared like no clear strategy. During this time, product development stalled as a deal was made with the outsourced product development vendor. It was decided to bring him in-house as the full-time technology lead while allowing him to retain interest in his primary business.

This conflict of interest was predicated by the fact that morale was declining and the well-intended, but at times overbearing, board intervened to attempt to get overly involved in personnel decisions within the operation of the company

The company amassed significant liabilities by the first quarter of 2021. Product development stalled and failed to meet evolving market needs. The technical lead focused more on his secondary venture as a protection mechanism to buffer what we felt was an eventual failure on the revenue end of the business.

The sales pipeline dried up and robust contracts were made with vendors that did not deliver results in lead generation and used haphazard investment in tools that brought no sales results, adding to the mounting financial problems. Their burn rate was rather large for a company of their size.

The rest of the team's motivation plummeted to an all-time low as the year closed out. Cash flow was waning, and cash on hand limited the company to 60 days of life and everyone feared the eventual collapse of the company.

This is when the angel investors reached out and recruited me to be the CEO. Nothing is ever as it seems, and the lesson in that is to always dig deep below the surface. If something appears too good to be true, it probably is.

The first six months were bumpy. I navigated a botched founder-to-CEO transition because what was portrayed to me, that the founder was on board, seemed not to be the case. That brought immediate tension and some tug of war since I had been given complete authorization to run the company. I can't say that there were no red flags in the beginning. The negotiation of my employment contract signaled the first of those red flags. Due to my insistence, it carved out an opportunity to exit the company equitably at some point.

We didn't hit our operating cadence until the third quarter, and then, for a majority of the year, from February through July, I kicked off a financing round and raised $2 million to keep the company afloat. We had pushed through operational efficiencies and stretched 60 days of capital to 90, and then to 120 days. The capital helped stabilize the company and the 71 percent increase in valuation did not hurt either.

I remember reaching out to a mentor after my third day in the position. I highlighted some of the red flags, the challenging tension between the founder and the CEO who had been selected to succeed him. I know that these things usually result in only one survivor in the long run. My mentor quickly reminded me of that.

His advice was that I had some options. I could parachute out right then. It might cause some embarrassment for the angel investor that brought me in, but it was survivable. Second, I could deliver on the capital raise, like he knew that I could, and then gracefully exit or take it in six-month increments. I opted for the wait and watch option to see how things evolved with the founder.

Unfortunately, the rough start and the pride and ego involved would not let things improve. I would realize that the emotional impact of the Founder transition to him was not going to get better. The support needed for my continued success was not there. The fit was not right. At many points throughout the year, I would think about how lucky I was to have gotten a new lease on life and how the most important people in my life were my family. After much soul searching towards the end of the year, the answer was glaring me in the face. This situation was not going to improve, so I had a limited number of options. In the end, I opted out at the thirteen-month mark.

I didn't have to prove anything to anyone. Pulling the company out of the flat tailspin it was in, was success in itself. Similar to my experience in navigating the yacht club through the first year of the pandemic, I knew that I could do it and I did. I really didn't need validation of my capabilities. It would have been nice, but it was not a need.

REFLECTION

I believe there isn't anything that we're given that we can't handle, and things are put in our way to allow us to grow, develop, flourish, and use our strengths. People are placed in our lives to teach us about ourselves and to genuinely allow us to see and learn. I value my SupplyHive experience as one of those things. I don't know if I went back in time that I would do it differently.

When you look back over every step and get to a vantage point where you can take a breath, even if it didn't go the way you hoped for, you can celebrate the successes of how far you've come. While 2021 was challenging, I can look back and see how far the company has come in a year. If you told me on January 20th, five days after I started, I probably would've given it a 50/50 chance of survival, but we made it. It's on the board at this time to take it the rest of the way. I'm cheering for them to succeed. I want them to succeed.

HEARTFELT GRATITUDE

When I'm driving a boat in a storm, I tell myself to steady the course and filter the noise. Only take the feedback that you need to drive the boat, and to drive it fast. Anything else is noise.

For me, that's my walk away point. I'm still at the helm of my life, and we're still rushing downwind in interesting seas. I don't know how this one's going to end, but I'm trying to stack it so it ends in the best way possible. At the end of the day, that's really all you can do in life. You live each day looking forward, understanding that you can look at the past or you can say it is what it is.

THAT'S WHERE THE GRATITUDE COMES IN

Who is Lou Sandoval? If you have made it this far, you will see that I am a compendium of the hopes and dreams of my grandparents, parents, and community. I have touched many lives and lived many experiences, much like we all have. I have been blessed to have met many wonderful people in my life so far, many who have been the little angels that have ushered my progress along the way. They have been my mentors, my sponsors, and spoke praises of me when I was not present. I am so humbly grateful for their grace and the impact that they have had on my life.

I've faced some interesting challenges–some that happened to me, and others that I happened upon. Some I could have read better. Some were self-inflicted, but that is life–it is imperfect.

I've had many successes and many failures. I am grateful for those failures because it is in failing that I have learned the most. I am profoundly grateful for those that have supported me and those who made my life difficult. It is in those difficulties that your purpose was fulfilled—to help me to grow.

I am a leader, a skilled operator of companies, adept at turning them around and driving change. My ridiculous comfort in navigating ambiguity and channeling a group of people to accomplish a goal, be it winning a boat race or succeeding in business, is a skill that I have worked hard at and continue to learn and improve upon, just as we all do. I am a work in progress.

My hope is that by reading my story, you are inspired to see that no matter what life throws at you, you can persevere. It will make sense; you just have to keep at it.

Who would have thought that a dyslexic, geeky, science loving, med-school dropout, cancer-surviving Hispanic kid from the South Side would have made it this far? Not many. The odds were not great at times. But I did and I have much road left ahead of me. As do you.

In my heart of hearts, I am an entrepreneur and a survivor.

It is my tenacity and willingness to play in that ambiguity and be an agent of change that fuels my passion–my tenacity for life.

On a recent visit to Stanford University, I was leaving a meeting and I happened to stumble on a quote just outside the business school from the founder of Nike, Mr. Phillip Knight.

The quote is cast inside an oval. At the top of the inside of the oval is a signature Nike waffle—soled left footprint.

Just outside of the oval is the complimentary right footprint. I share it with you below so that you, too, can step into that uncertainty—armed with your own tenacity for life.

Dedication from Philip H. Knight - Stanford Graduate School of Business

"There comes a time in every life when the past recedes and the future opens. It's that moment when you turn to face the unknown. Some will turn back to what they already know. Some will walk straight ahead into uncertainty. I can't tell you which one is right. But I can tell you which one is more fun." - Philip H. Knight (Stanford MBA 1962)

ABOUT THE AUTHOR

Lou Sandoval is the president and managing partner of Halo Advisory Group, a management consulting firm working with start-ups to Fortune 100 companies to drive digital transformation and the application of technology to improve operating efficiency at scale.

Most recently, Lou served as president and CEO of SupplyHive™, a software technology company based in Chicago that serves Fortune 500 clients in the development of their supplier performance and diversity metrics. Previously, he held senior leadership positions at Brunswick Corporation, a global consumer goods company based in the Chicago area.

Lou has served on the Wintrust Bank board of directors since 2015 where he chairs the risk management committee and serves on nominating, compensation, and governance.

He brings more than 30 years of professional experience in business development, mergers and acquisitions, technology, and leading strategic growth initiatives. His board service extends to the non-profit sector as well, with over two decades of service on various local and national boards.

Many Fortune 100 companies have trusted Lou to lead technology-driven organizational transformations in consumer engagement with health care, business services, durable consumer products, and industrial products. His diverse background gives him a unique vantage point of many market verticals and has made him a valuable advisor to many companies.

Lou also serves on the advisory board of two early-stage startups in satellite communications and marine technology, and has held leadership positions on the Boy Scouts of America board of directors. He is also on the 145-year-old Chicago Yacht Club's board of directors, where he also served as the sixty-ninth commodore and chairman of the board. In addition, he serves on the board of trustees for Epic Academy, a Charter High School in the South Chicago neighborhood where he grew up.

Together with his wife and two daughters, Lou lives on Chicago's South Side. In his spare time, Sandoval is a competitive offshore sailor, having navigated over 30,000 nautical miles and won the storied Chicago Yacht Club Race to Mackinac nine times. In 2021, he was inducted into the Lake Michigan Sailing Hall of Fame.

Made in United States
Orlando, FL
30 April 2022

17352490R00183